The Impact of Computers on Society and Ethics: A Bibliography

The Impact of Computers on Society and Ethics: A Bibliography

Edited by Gary M. Abshire

Creative Computing
Morristown, New Jersey

Copyright © 1980 by Creative Computing

All rights reserved. No portion of this book may be reproduced - mechanically, electronically or by any other means, including photocopying - without written permission of the publisher.

Library of Congress No. 80-65696
ISBN 0-916688-17-8

Printed in the United States of America
First printing June 1980

10 9 8 7 6 5 4 3 2 1

Creative Computing Press
P.O. Box 789-M
Morristown, NJ 07960

Foreword

Computers are machines that can perform computations in seconds that would take humans hundreds of years to accomplish. They can perform with unerring accuracy second after second, hour after hour. Furthermore, the computer is a universal machine. Any calculation that can be done by any other machine can be done by a computer.

A computer is a tool controlled by humans that enables one to perform many complex calculations in a very short time, keep track of various business transactions, teach pilots to land aircraft by simulating the changing appearance of landing fields, aid doctors by analyzing signals from diagnostic instruments, and do thousands of other tasks that were unheard of a few years ago.

The physical equipment of a computer system may weigh less than a pound or more than a ton, cost less than $100 or more than a $100 million, and fit into your hand or occupy many rooms in different cities.

But, where is the computer leading us? Is the computer a menace or a messiah? What are the benefits of computers? What are the risks? What is needed to manage the computer for society's greatest good? What is society's greatest good? Will we become the masters or the slaves of the evolving computer technology? Is there a comfortable position in between master and slave for us?

This bibliography was created to help you answer these questions. The works cited can help you make up your mind on the issues of central importance to the future of the individual and society. The computer will have that much effect on our lives.

This bibliography contains a list of books, magazine articles, news items, scholarly papers, and other works dealing with computers and their impact on our society and ethics. A few entries are not about computers, but are included because of their usefulness as background information. Given are 1920 references in alphabetical order with comments appended to some of the entries. Material from 1948 through 1979 is included.

This bibliography includes titles of works dealing with the ways in which computers are being used in our society, the beneficial changes that are taking place in our lives as a result of computer technology, the social and ethical problems intensified by the improper use of computers, the dangers of a computerized society, the safeguards and defenses against those dangers, the attempts to indicate what computerized direction the future will take, and the responsibilities of computer professionals.

Books of Interest

Readers interested in the role of the computer in society will also want to subscribe to Creative Computing magazine, the #1 applications and software magazine. Subscriptions in the USA cost $15 per year, $28 for two years and $40 for three years. Subscribers in Canada and Mexico must add $4 per year, and those in other foreign countries must add $9 per year additional postage. A sample copy is $2.50 anywhere.

Creative Computing also publishes a wide selection of other books. If they are not available locally they may be ordered directly from the publisher. Please add $1.00 shipping charge for each book ordered, $2.00 for 2 or more books. New Jersey residents add 5% sales tax. For foreign orders add $2.00 for each book. A catalog for Creative Computing Press is available free upon request.

The Best of Creative Computing-Volume I—Ahl	$8.95
The Best of Creative Computing-Volume II—Ahl	$8.95
The Best of Creative Computing-Volume III—Ahl & Green	$8.95
The Best of Byte—Ahl & Helmers	$11.95
Computers in Mathematics: A Sourcebook of Ideas—Ahl	$15.95
Basic Computer Games—Ahl	$7.50
More Basic Computer Games—Ahl & North	$7.50
Problems for Computer Solution—Rogowski	$4.95
Problems for Computer Solution: Teacher's Edition—Rogowski	$9.95
Computer Coin Games—Weisbecker	$3.95
Be a Computer Literate—Ball & Charp	$3.95
Katie and the Computer—D'Ignazio & Gilliam	$6.95
Tales of the Marvelous Machine: Thirty-five Stories of Computing—Taylor & Green	$7.95
The Colossal Computer Cartoon Book—Ahl	$4.95
Artist and Computer—Leavitt	$4.95
Computer Music Festival Record	$6.00
Computer Rage Game	$8.95

Creative Computing Press
P.O. Box 789-M
Morristown, NJ 07960

Abbreviations and Acronyms

ACM	Association for Computing Machinery
AFIPS	American Federation of Information Processing Societies
CAI	Computer-Assisted Instruction
CAM	Computer-Assisted Manufacturing
CBEMA	Computer and Business Equipment Manufacturing Association
CMI	Computer-Managed Instruction
DP	Data Processing
ed.	editor
EDP	Electronic Data Processing
eds.	editors
EFT	Electronic Funds Transfer
EFTS	Electronic Funds Transfer System
FCC	Federal Communications Commission
FJCC	Fall Joint Computer Conference
IBM	International Business Machines
IEEE	Institute of Electrical and Electronics Engineers
IRE	Institute of Radio Engineers
LEAA	Law Enforcement Assistance Administration
MIS	Management Information Systems
MIT	Massachusetts Institute of Technology
no.	number
nos.	numbers
OECD	Organization for Economic Cooperation and Development
p.	page
POS	Point of Sale
pp.	pages
SDC	System Development Corporation
SIGCSE	Special Interest Group on Computer Science Education
SJCC	Spring Joint Computer Conference
UPC	Universal Product Code
vol.	volume

Bibliography

"A Bill to Prevent the Invasion of Privacy Through the Misuse of Computer Information." Computers and Automation, vol. 18, no. 7, July 1969, pp. 13-14.

"A Complete Interview for Emergency Room Patients." Computers and Biomedical Research, vol. 6, no. 3, June 1973, pp. 257-265.

A National Survey of the Public's Attitudes Toward Computers. AFIPS-Time, 1972, 58 pp. Results based on 1,001 telephone interviews.

Aaron, Harold R., and Campbell, Robert P. "Computer Security - Not a Hopeless Task." Government Executive, vol. 9, no. 5, May 1977, pp. 58-64.

Abbatt, F.R., and others. "Computer-Based Learning in the Physical Sciences." Physics Education, vol. 7, no. 3, March 1972, pp. 136-141.

Abbott, William. "Work in the Year 2001." Current, no. 193, May-June 1977, pp. 31-38. From "Work in the Year 2001," The Futurist, February 1977, pp. 25-31.

Abboud, Victorine. "The Computer as an Instructional Device for the Arabic Writing System." Computers and the Humanities, vol. 6, no. 4, March 1972, pp. 195-207.

Abdian, A.G., and Klienfelter, P. "Transfer of Security-Classified Information." Journal of Chemical Documentation, November 1970, pp. 224-226.

Abell, Bruce. "A Technology Assessment: The Social Consequences of Far Less Cash and Checks." Computers and People, vol. 26, no. 2, February 1977, pp. 7-10, 21.

Abelson, Robert P. "Computers, Polls, and Public Opinion - Some Puzzles and Paradoxes." Trans-Action, September 1968, pp. 20-27.

Abrams, M.E., ed. Medical Computing. New York, New York: Elsevier-North Holland, 1970, 396 pp.

Abshire, Gary M. "Ethics, Society, and Computers - A Bibliography." Lafayette, Louisiana: University of Southwestern Louisiana, Computer Science Department, Report 77-8-1, 26 August 1977, 44 pp. About 490 references in year-date sequence starting with 1954 and ending in mid 1977.

_____. "Ethics, Society, and Computers - Some Quotations." Lafayette, Louisiana: University of Southwestern Louisiana, Computer Science Department, Report 78-8-1, 11 January 1978, 30 pp. About 160 quotations on responsibilities, prophecies, and consequences.

──────. "CMPS 300, Computers and Modern Society: A Course in Computer Literacy." Lafayette, Louisiana: University of Southwestern Louisiana, Computer Science Department, Report 78-8-2, 8 May 1978, 27 pp. Description of a course given during the 1977-78 academic year; includes the uncorrelated responses of a questionnaire on students' attitudes toward computers.

──────. "Computer-Assisted Instruction: A Supplement to Traditional Instruction." Boulder, Colorado: IBM Corporation, Technical Report 77.0038, 2 January 1979, 21 pp.

Abt, Clark C. "The Social Role of Technology." *Educational Technology*, vol. 13, no. 8, August 1973, pp. 20-22.

Ackley, G. "Automation: Threat and Promise." *New York Times Magazine*, 22 March 1964, p. 16.

Ackoff, Russell L. "Management Misinformation Systems." *Management Science*, vol. 14, no. 4, December 1967, pp. 147-156.

──────., ed. *Designing a National Scientific and Technological Communication System*. Philadelphia, Pennsylvania: University of Pennsylvania Press, 1976.

ACM. *Computers in the Service of Man*. New York, New York: August 1973, 458 pp. Proceedings of ACM's Annual Conference, Atlanta, Georgia.

──────. *Computers and the Quality of Life*. New York, New York: 20-22 October 1975, 372 pp. Proceedings of ACM's Annual Conference, Minneapolis, Minnesota.

──────. *Privacy, Security and the Information Processing Industry*. New York, New York: January 1976, 200 pp. Report of ACM's Ombudsman Committee on Privacy, Los Angeles, California.

Adams, Carl A. "BankAmericard Assesses Electronic Value Exchange." In *Computer Technology to Reach the People: Digest of Papers*, pp. 167-168. New York, New York: The Institute of Electrical and Electronics Engineers, Inc., Spring COMPCON75, IEEE Catalog No. 75CH0920-9C, February 1975.

Adams, E.N. "Roles of the Electronic Computer in University Instruction." Yorktown Heights, New York: IBM Corporation, Report RC-1530, October 1965, 14 pp.

──────. "A Proposed Computer Controlled Language Laboratory." Yorktown Heights, New York: IBM Corporation, Report RC-1558, March 1966, 8 pp.

──────. "Reflections on the Design of a CAI Operating System." Yorktown Heights, New York: IBM Corporation, Report RC-1745, January 1967.

──────. "Use of CAI in Foreign Language Instruction." Yorktown Heights, New York: IBM Corporation, Report RC-2377, 30 October 1968, 6 pp.

_____. "Computer-Based Instruction and Management in Foreign Language Teaching: A Systems Concept." Yorktown Heights, New York: IBM Corporation, Report RC-2658, 8 October 1969, 22 pp.

_____. "The Computer in Academic Instruction." Yorktown Heights, New York: IBM Corporation, Report RC-3063, September 1970, 18 pp.

Adams, E.N., and Morrison, H.W. "Pilot Study of a CAI Laboratory in German." Modern Language Journal, vol. 52, no. 5, May 1968, pp. 279-287.

Adams, E.N.; Morrison, H.W.; and Reddy, J.M. "Conversation with a Computer as a Technique of Language Instruction." Modern Language Journal, vol. 52, no. 1, January 1968, pp. 3-16.

Adams, E.N., and Quinn, E.M. "Automation of Prescription in an Individual Progress Instruction System." Yorktown Heights, New York: IBM Corporation, Report RC-2406, March 1969, 10 pp. Learning assignments.

Adams, J. Mack, and Haden, Douglas H. Computers: Appreciation, Applications, Implications - An Introduction. New York, New York: John Wiley and Sons, 1973, 584 pp.

_____. Social Effects of Computer Use and Misuse. New York, New York: John Wiley and Sons, 1976.

Adams, Sexton. "EDP Effects on Organization Structure." Business Review, Winter 1966-67, pp. 16-27.

Adelson, Alan M. "Whir, Blink, Jackpot! - Crooked Operators Use Computers to Embezzle Money from Computers." The Wall Street Journal, 5 April 1968, p. 1.

_____. "Computer Bandits." True, February 1969, pp. 50, 74, 76, 77.

Ahl, David H. Getting Started in Classroom Computing. Maynard, Massachusetts: Digital Equipment Corporation, 1974, 29 pp.

_____., ed. The Best of Creative Computing, Volume 1. Morristown, New Jersey: Creative Computing Press, 1976, 317 pp.

_____. "Can Computers Think?" Creative Computing, March-April 1976, pp. 20-24.

_____., ed. The Best of Creative Computing, Volume 2. Morristown, New Jersey: Creative Computing Press, 1977.

_____. The Colossal Computer Cartoon Book. Morristown, New Jersey: Creative Computing Press, 1977.

Ahl, David H., and Bailey, James. "Computers Are for Kids - Not for Geniuses." School Management, vol. 15, no. 4, April 1971, pp. 26-28.

Aiken, Henry. *Reason and Conduct*. New York, New York: Alfred A. Knopf, 1962.

Albert, Ethel M. "The Classification of Values: A Method and Illustration." *American Anthropologist*, April 1956, pp. 221-248.

_____. "'First Principles' in Logic and Ethics." *Bucknell Review*, vol. 7, no. 3, March 1958, pp. 133-143.

_____. *Great Traditions in Ethics: An Introduction*. Florence, Kentucky: D. Van Nostrand, 1975.

Albus, James S. "The Economics of the Robot Revolution." *Analog*, vol. 95, no. 4, April 1975, pp. 70-81. Reader comment in *Analog*, vol. 95, no. 8, August 1975, pp. 171-176.

_____. "Automation and the Sleeping Nation." *Computer Decisions*, vol. 7, no. 8, August 1975, pp. 28, 31-32, 34.

_____. *Peoples' Capitalism: The Economics of the Robot Revolution*. Kensington, Maryland: New World Books, 1976.

Albus, James S., and Evans, John M., Jr. "Robot Systems." *Scientific American*, vol. 234, no. 2, February 1976, pp. 76-86B. The use of robots in factories.

Alderman, Donald L., and Anastasio, Ernest J. "Computers and Education." *Computers and Society*, Summer 1974, pp. 3-5.

Alderman, Tom. "Computer Crime." *Journal of Systems Management*, vol. 28, no. 9, September 1977, pp. 32-35.

Alexander, Tom. "Computers Can't Solve Everything." *Fortune*, vol. 80, no. 5, October 1969, pp. 126-129, 168, 171.

_____. "Waiting for the Great Computer Rip-Off." *Fortune*, July 1974, pp. 143-146, 148, 150.

_____. *Social Values: Objectives and Action*. New York, New York: Halsted Press, 1975.

Alger, Philip L., and others. *Ethical Problems in Engineering*. New York, New York: John Wiley and Sons, 1965.

Algie, Jimmy, and Hall, Anthony S. "A Work Game for Social Services." *Simulation*, vol. 21, no. 6, December 1973, pp. 166-176.

Allan, J.A. "Embezzlement by Electronics." *Accountants Magazine*, April 1960, pp. 253-255.

Allderige, J.M. "Off-Line Management." *Datamation*, vol. 14, no. 6, June 1968, pp. 43-46.

Allen, Brandt R. "Danger Ahead! Safeguard Your Computer." *Harvard Business Review*, vol. 46, no. 6, November-December 1968, pp. 97-101.

_____. "Computer Fraud." _Financial Executive_, May 1971, pp. 38-44.

_____. "Computer Security - Part 1." _Data Management_, vol. 10, no. 1, January 1972, pp. 18-24.

_____. "Computer Security - Part 2." _Data Management_, vol. 10, no. 2, February 1972, pp. 24-30.

_____. "Embezzler's Guide to the Computer." _Harvard Business Review_, vol. 53, no. 4, July-August 1975, pp. 79-89.

_____. "Embezzlement and Automation." In _Computers - The Next 5 Years: Digest of Papers_, pp. 187-188. New York, New York: The Institute of Electrical and Electronics Engineers, Inc., Spring COMPCON76, IEEE Catalog No. 76CH1069-4(CR), February 1976.

_____. "The Biggest Computer Frauds: Lessons for CPAs." _Journal of Accountancy_, May 1977, pp. 52-62.

Allen, John R. "Two Routines for Use in CAI Language Programs." _Computers and the Humanities_, vol. 6, no. 2, November 1971, pp. 125-128.

_____. "Current Trends in Computer-Assisted Instruction." _Computers and the Humanities_, vol. 7, no. 1, September 1972, pp. 47-54.

_____. "The Cybernetic Centaur: Advances in Computer-Assisted Instruction." _Computers and the Humanities_, vol. 7, no. 6, September-November 1973, pp. 373-387.

Allvin, R.L. "Computer-Assisted Music Instruction: A Look at the Potential." Los Gatos, California: IBM Corporation, Report 16.164, September 1968, 16 pp.

Alpert, Daniel, and Bitzer, Donald L. "Advances in Computer-Based Education." _Science_, vol. 167, no. 3925, 20 March 1970, pp. 1582-1590.

Alter, Steven L. "How Effective Managers Use Information Systems." _Harvard Business Review_, vol. 54, no. 6, November-December 1976, pp. 97-104.

_____. "Why is Man-Computer Interaction Important for Decision-Support Systems?" _Interfaces_, vol. 7, no. 2, February 1977, pp. 109-115.

Amara, Roy. _Toward Understanding the Social Impact of Computers_. Menlo Park, California: Institute for the Future, 1974.

Amdahl, Lowell. "Computer Obsolescence." _Datamation_, vol. 15, no. 1, January 1969, pp. 27-28.

Amosov, Nicolai M. _Modeling of Thinking and the Mind_. New York, New York: Spartan Books, 1967.

Amstutz, Arnold E. _Computer Simulation of Competitive Market Response_. Cambridge, Massachusetts: MIT Press, 1967.

"Analysis of Enacted EFTS State Legislation." _Modern Data_, January 1976, pp. 27-29.

Anderson, A., Jr. "Forecast for Forecasting: Cloudy." _The New York Times Magazine_, 29 December 1974, pp. 10-31. Weather forecasting by computer.

Anderson, Alan R., ed. _Minds and Machines_. Englewood Cliffs, New Jersey: Prentice-Hall Publishers, 1964.

Anderson, Ernest G. "CAI: The State of the Art." _Nation's Schools_, vol. 82, no. 4, October 1968, pp. 48-51.

Anderson, Howard. "Computer-Based Message System." _The Office_, vol. 88, no. 5, November 1978, pp. 134, 136.

Anderson, Jack. "Computer Experts Could Easily Tap Government Secrets." _Rocky Mountain News_, 20 May 1976, p. 6.

Anderson, Norman G. "Science and Management Techniques." _Computers and Society_, Spring 1974, pp. 4-5.

Anderson, Robert H. "Programmable Automation: The Bright Future of Computers in Manufacturing." _Datamation_, vol. 18, no. 12, December 1972, pp. 46-52.

Anderson, Ronald E. "Sociological Analysis of Public Attitudes Toward Computers and Information Files." _AFIPS Conference Proceedings_, SJCC, vol. 40, 16-18 May 1972, pp. 649-657.

_____. "Bibliography on Social Science Computing." _Computing Reviews_, vol. 15, no. 7, July 1974, pp. 247-261.

_____. "Value Orientation of Computer Science Students." _Communications of the ACM_, vol. 21, no. 3, March 1978, pp. 219-225.

Anderson, Ronald E., and Fagerlund, Ed. "Privacy and the Computer: An Annotated Bibliography." _Computing Reviews_, November 1972, pp. 551-559.

Andreski, Stanislav. _Social Science as Sorcery_. New York, New York: St. Martin's Press, 1973.

Angel, Edward, and others. "Computers in Obstetrics." In _Digest of Papers_, pp. 318-321. New York, New York: The Institute of Electrical and Electronics Engineers, Inc., Fall COMPCON76, IEEE Catalog No. 76CH1115-5C, September 1976.

Anonsen, Sheldon Lee. "Interactive Computer Graphics in Architecture." _Computers and Automation_, vol. 19, no. 8, August 1970, pp. 27-30.

Anshen, Melvin. "Manager and the Black Box." Harvard Business Review, vol. 39, no. 6, November-December 1960, pp. 85-92.

_____., ed. Managing the Socially Responsible Corporation. New York, New York: The Macmillan Company, 1974.

Ansoff, H. Igor. "Making Effective Use of Computers in Managerial Decision Making." Automation, October 1967, pp. 68-73.

Appleton, Daniel S. "A Strategy for Manufacturing Automation." Datamation, vol. 23, no. 10, October 1977, pp. 64-68, 70.

Appleton, Jon H., and Perera, Ronald C., eds. The Development and Practice of Electronic Music. Englewood Cliffs, New Jersey: Prentice-Hall, Inc., 1975.

Arbib, Michael A. The Metaphorical Brain: An Introduction to Cybernetics As Artificial Intelligence and Brain Theory. New York, New York: Wiley-Interscience, 1972.

_____. "Man-Machine Symbiosis and the Evolution of Human Freedom." American Scholar, vol. 43, no. 1, Winter 1973-74, pp. 38-54.

_____. Computers and the Cybernetic Society. New York, New York: Academic Press, 1977, 494 pp.

"Are You Afraid of a Computer?" Senior Scholastic, 20 September 1973, pp. 14-15.

Argyris, Chris. "Management Information Systems: The Challenge to Rationality and Emotionality." Management Science, vol. 17, no. 6, February 1971, pp. 275-291.

Arleigh, Robert. "Could You Be Sued for Invasion of Privacy?" Medical Economics, 2 April 1973, pp. 78-83.

Armer, Paul. "Attitudes Toward Intelligent Machines." Datamation, vol. 9, no. 3, March 1963, pp. 34-38.

_____. "Social Implications of the Computer Utility." Santa Monica, California: The RAND Corporation, Report P-3642, August 1967.

_____. "The Individual: His Privacy, Self-Image, and Obsolescence." Computers and People, vol. 24, no. 6, June 1975, pp. 18-23.

_____. "Computer Technology and Surveillance." Computers and People, vol. 24, no. 9, September 1975, pp. 8-11.

Arnett, Edward M. "Computer-Based Chemical Information Services." Science, 25 December 1970, pp. 1370-1376.

Arnett, Edward M., and Kent, Allen, eds. Computer Based Chemical Information. New York, New York: Mercel Dekker, Inc., 1973.

Arnold, Ron, and Penny, Ruth. "Who Should Write CAI Curriculum?" Educational Technology, vol. 9, no. 10, October 1969, pp. 88-91.

Aron, Joel D. "Real-Time Systems in Perspective." *IBM Systems Journal*, vol. 6, no. 1, 1967, pp. 49-67.

_____. "Information Systems in Perspective." *Computing Surveys*, vol. 1, no. 4, December 1969, pp. 213-236.

Aronoff, Stanley J. "1984 - Only 11 Years Away: How the States Can Help Prevent the Orwellian Prediction." *State Government*, vol. 46, no. 2, Spring 1973, pp. 66-75.

Arup, Jens, and Scott, T.G. "What Can You Do with Computers?" *New University*, vol. 3, no. 7, November 1969, pp. 19-20.

Arzell, L. "A Superintendent's View of a Computer System." *School Management*, vol. 15, no. 12, December 1971, pp. 12-14.

Asbell, B. *The New Improved American*. New York, New York: McGraw-Hill Book Company, 1963.

Ascher, Marcia. "Computers in Science Fiction." *Harvard Business Review*, December 1963, pp. 40-42, 44, 46, 50, 188, 190, 192.

Ashby, W. Ross. *An Introduction to Cybernetics*. New York, New York: Barnes and Nobel, 1956.

Asimov, Isaac. *I, Robot*. Garden City, New York: Doubleday and Company, 1963. Science fiction.

_____. "And It Will Serve Us Right." *Psychology Today*, vol. 2, no. 11, April 1969, pp. 39-40, 64.

Asten, Kenneth J. *Data Communication for Business Information Systems*. New York, New York: The Macmillan Company, 1973.

Atkinson, Richard C., and Fletcher, John D. "Teaching Children to Read with a Computer." *Reading Teacher*, vol. 25, no. 4, January 1972, pp. 319-327.

Atkinson, Richard C., and Wilson, H.A., eds. *Computer-Assisted Instruction: A Book of Readings*. New York, New York: Academic Press, 1969, 362 pp.

Auerbach, Alexander. "Talking Back to Machines." *Saturday Review of the Society*, March 1973, pp. 62-63.

Austen, Alfred. "Major Role for Mini Computers." *Marketing*, October 1976, pp. 16-19, 60.

Austing, Richard H., and Engel, Gerald L. *A Study of Computer Impact on Society and Computer Literacy Courses and Materials*. (Also entitled *An Annotated Bibliography on Computer Impact on Society*.) Virginia Institute of Marine Science, 30 June 1976, 482 pp. Approximately 2000 references.

Austrian, Geoffrey D. "Privacy and Data Security." *Think*, March 1974, pp. 10-17.

_____. "Big Stakes." *Think*, July-August 1977, pp. 4-9. FCC looks at where data processing leaves off and communications begin.

"Automatic Fire Protection System Protects Continental's EDP Units." *Insurance*, 1 March 1970, p. 36. Continental Airline's carbon dioxide extinguishing system.

Autry, Vaughn M. "Computer: Boon or Downfall?" *Data Management*, vol. 12, no. 1, January 1974, pp. 26-28.

Avorn, Jerry. "The Future of Doctoring." *Atlantic*, November 1974, pp. 71-79.

Awad, Elias M. "The Dilemma of the System Analyst." *Computers and Automation*, vol. 19, no. 8, August 1970, pp. 34-38.

_____. *Business Data Processing*. 4th edition. Englewood Cliffs, New Jersey: Prentice-Hall, Inc., 1975, 722 pp.

_____. "The Issue of Electronic Funds Transfer: An Overview and Perspective." *Computers and People*, vol. 26, no. 6, June 1977, pp. 7-9, 22.

Awad, Elias M., and Data Processing Management Association. *Automatic Data Processing: Principles and Procedures*. 3rd edition. Englewood Cliffs, New Jersey: Prentice-Hall, Inc., 1973.

Bacot, Eugene. "Trapping Data Bank Busters." *Business Administration*, January 1971, pp. 16-19.

Baer, Robert M. *The Digital Villain: Notes on the Numerology, Parapsychology, and Metaphysics of the Computer*. Reading, Massachusetts: Addison-Wesley Publishing Company, 1972, 187 pp.

Bagdikian, Ben H. *The Information Machines: Their Impact on Men and the Media*. New York, New York: Harper and Row, Publishers, 1971.

Bagley, Barbara J. "Computer Applications: Nine Cases." *Traffic Management*, vol. 17, no. 6, June 1978, pp. 46-52.

Baier, Kurt. *The Moral Point of View: A Rational Basis of Ethics*. New York, New York: Random House, 1968.

Bailey, R.W. *Computer Poems*. Drummond Island, Michigan: Potagannissing Press, 1973.

Bain, Harry. "Privacy: What's Happening to a Fundamental Right?" *SDC Magazine*, vol. 10, no. 7, July-August 1967, pp. 1-24.

Baker, Frank B. *Computer-Managed Instruction: Theory and Practice*. Englewood Cliffs, New Jersey: Educational Technology Publishers, Inc., 1978.

Baker, W.O., and others. "Computers and Research." *Science*, vol. 195, no. 4283, 18 March 1977, pp. 1134-1139.

Balderston, F.E.; Carman, James M.; and Hoggatt, Austin C. "Computers in Banking and Marketing." *Science*, vol. 195, no. 4283, 18 March 1977, pp. 1115-1119.

Ball, Marion J. *Selecting a Computer System for the Clinical Laboratory*. Springfield, Illinois: Charles C. Thomas, Publisher, 1971.

―――., ed. *How to Select a Computerized Hospitial Information System*. White Plains, New York: S. Karger, 1973.

―――. "Computers: Prescription for Hospital Ills." *Datamation*, vol. 21, no. 9, September 1975, pp. 50-51.

Ball, Vaughn C. "The Impact of Data-Processing Technology on the Legal Profession." *Computers and Automation*, vol. 17, no. 4, April 1968, pp. 43-47.

Balls, Herbert R. "Developing a Canadian Electronic Payments System: The Federal Government's Interest and Involvement." *Optimum*, vol. 9, no. 1, 1978, pp. 43-60.

Balte, A.J., and Machlup, S. "Instructional Uses of the Computer: Orbiting Satellites for the Elementary Laboratory." *American Journal of Physics*, vol. 39, no. 3, March 1971, p. 333.

"Banks May Face Trouble with DP Disasters." *Data Management*, vol. 9, no. 5, May 1971, pp. 46-47.

Banzhaf, John F., III. "When Your Computer Needs a Lawyer." *Communications of the ACM*, vol. 11, no. 8, August 1968, pp. 543-549. Liability for negligence, torts, and warranties.

Baram, Michael S. "Technology Assessment and Social Control." *Science*, vol. 180, 4 May 1973, pp. 465-473.

Baran, Paul. "Communications, Computers and People." *AFIPS Conference Proceedings*, FJCC, vol. 27, Part 2, November-December 1965, pp. 45-49.

―――. "Remarks on the Question of Privacy Raised by the Automation of Mental Health Records." Santa Monica, California: The RAND Corporation, Report P-3523, April 1967.

―――. "The Future Computer Utility." *The Public Interest*, vol. 8, Summer 1967, pp. 75-87.

Bare, C.E. "The Measurement of Attitudes Toward Man-Machine Systems." *Human Factors*, February 1966, pp. 71-79.

Barna, Becky. "Ford's Privacy Report." *Computer Decisions*, vol. 9, no. 2, February 1977, pp. 27-30.

_____. "The DP Industry: The Next Five Years." Computer Decisions, vol. 10, no. 1, January 1978, pp. 48-51.

_____. "Electronic Messaging Can Make Cents." Computer Decisions, vol. 10, no. 9, September 1978, pp. 34, 36-38, 40, 42.

_____. "Cleaning Up the Federal DP Mess." Computer Decisions, vol. 10, no. 12, December 1978, pp. 34-35, 38, 40, 42.

Barnes, Dennis O., and Finkelstein, Arlene. "The Role of Computer-Assisted Instruction at the National Institute for the Deaf." American Annals of the Deaf, vol. 116, no. 5, October 1971, pp. 469-472.

Barth, J. Giles Goat-Boy, or the Revised, New Syllabus. New York, New York: Doubleday and Company, 1966.

Barton, Walter E. "Should a National Commission for the Preservation of Confidentiality of Health Records be Formed?" Psychiatric Opinion, January 1975, pp. 15-17.

Bassler, Richard A. "EDP Professionals and Certification." Journal of Data Education, October 1976, pp. 11-14.

Bassler, Richard A., and Enger, N.L. Computer Systems and Public Administrators. Arlington, Virginia: College Readings, 1976.

Bassler, Richard A., and Joslin, Edward O. Applications of Computer Systems. Arlington, Virginia: College Readings, 1974.

Bates, Nataniel B. "The Computer: Is It a Gimmick?" Independent School Bulletin, vol. 29, no. 4, May 1970, pp. 51-52.

Bates, William S. "Security of Computer-Based Information Systems." Datamation, vol. 16, no. 5, May 1970, pp. 60-65.

Bauer, Raymond A. "Societal Feedback." The Annals of the American Academy of Political and Social Science, September 1967, pp. 181-188.

Baxter, W.P.C., and Scott, K.E. Retail Banking in the Electronic Age: The Law and Economics of Electronic Funds Transfer. Montclair, New Jersey: Allanheld Osmun, 1977.

Baynard, Ernest C. "Computers in the Congress." Honeywell Computer Journal, vol. 6, no. 4, 1972, pp. 261-273.

Beardsley, C.W. "Is Your Computer Insecure?" IEEE Spectrum, January 1972, pp. 67-78.

Bearse, R.C., and Maxwell, B.D. "Development and Implementation of a Faculty Interest Database." Journal of the Society of Research Administration, vol. 9, no. 3, Winter 1978, pp. 9-13.

Beck, Robert N. "The Right of Professional Privacy." The Personalist, vol. 55, no. 2, Spring 1974, pp. 145-150.

Becker, Joseph. "Information Network Prospects in the United States." <u>Library Trends</u>, vol. 17, January 1969, pp. 306-317.

_____., ed. <u>Interlibrary Communications and Information Networks</u>. Chicago, Illinois: American Library Association, 1972.

Beckwith, B.P. <u>The Next Five Hundred Years</u>. New York, New York: Exposition Press, 1967.

Beeler, Jeffry. "Edwin Newman Gives DP Jargon Passing Grade." <u>Computerworld</u>, vol. 12, no. 50, 11 December 1978, pp. 1, 7.

Behrens, Carl. "Computers and Security." <u>Science News</u>, vol. 91, 3 June 1967, pp. 532-533.

Belden, T.G., and Belden, M.R. <u>The Lengthening Shadow: The Life of Thomas J. Watson</u>. Boston, Massachusetts: Little, Brown and Company, 1962.

Bell, C. Gordon; Chen, Robert; and Rege, Satish. "Effect of Technology on Near-Term Computer Structures." <u>Computer</u>, March-April 1972, pp. 29-38.

Bell, Daniel. <u>The Management of Information and Knowledge</u>. Washington, D.C.: United States House of Representatives, Committee on Science and Astronautics, 1970.

_____. "Technology, Nature and Society: The Vicissitudes of Three World Views and the Confusion of Realms." <u>American Scholar</u>, Summer 1973, pp. 385-404.

_____. <u>The Coming of Post-Industrial Society</u>. New York, New York: Basic Books, Inc., 1976.

_____. "Teletext and Technology: New Networks of Knowledge and Information in Post-Industrial Society." <u>Encounter</u>, June 1977, pp. 9-29.

Bellamy, C.J., and Race, D. "Computers and Medicine." <u>Australian Computer Journal</u>, vol. 1, no. 2, May 1968, pp. 78-81.

Bemer, Robert W., ed. <u>Computers and Crisis: How Computers Are Shaping Our Future</u>. New York, New York: Petrocelli/Charter, 1971. Proceedings of ACM's Annual Conference, New York, New York, August 1970.

_____. "The Frictional Interface between Computers and Society." <u>Computers and People</u>, vol. 26, no. 1, January 1975, pp. 14-19.

Ben-David, Joseph. <u>The Scientist's Role in Society</u>. Englewood Cliffs, New Jersey: Prentice-Hall, Inc., 1971.

Benford, Gregory, and Book, David. "Promise-Child in the Land of the Humans." <u>Smithsonian</u>, April 1971, pp. 58-65.

Bennett, J.M. "Computers and the Visual Arts." <u>Australian Computer Journal</u>, vol. 3, no. 4, November 1971, pp. 171-177.

Bentley, T.J. "Auditability and Control of Computers." *Management Accounting*, vol. 55, no. 1, January 1977, pp. 13-14.

Benton, John B. "Economic Value and EFT - 'Rationality or Speculation.'" In *Digest of Papers*, pp. 120-122. New York, New York: The Institute of Electrical and Electronics Engineers, Inc., Spring COMPCON76, IEEE Catalog No. 76CH1069-4(CR), February 1976.

_____. "Electronic Funds Transfer: Pitfall and Payoffs." *Harvard Business Review*, vol. 55, no. 4, July-August 1977, pp. 16-17, 20, 22, 28-29, 32, 164, 166, 168, 170, 172-173.

Benton, Myron. *The Privacy Invaders*. New York, New York: Coward-McCann, 1964.

Berg, John L. "Federal Privacy Act Countdown...Is the Private Sector Ready?" *Infosystems*, vol. 22, no. 2, July 1975, pp. 25-26.

Berger, Melvin. *Those Amazing Computers*. New York, New York: John Day Company, 1973.

Berger, R. "Cheap Labor: The Personal Computer." *Working Woman*, vol. 3, October 1978, pp. 60-61.

Berk, Toby S. "Myths About Computers." *Computers and Society*, Winter 1975, pp. 3-5.

Berkeley, Edmund C. *Giant Brains or Machines that Think*. New York, New York: John Wiley and Sons, 1949.

_____. *The Computer Revolution*. New York, New York: Doubleday and Company, 1962.

_____. "Individual Privacy and Central Computerized Files." *Computers and Automation*, vol. 15, no. 10, October 1966, p. 7. Editorial.

_____. "Professional Conduct in the Computer Field." *Computers and Automation*, vol. 16, no. 9, September 1967, p. 7. Editorial.

_____. "Computer-Assisted Explanation." *Computers and Automation*, vol. 16, no. 9, September 1967, pp. 32-37.

_____. "Computers and Moral Questions." *Computers and Automation*, vol. 17, no. 3, March 1968, pp. 7, 46. Editorial.

_____. "The Misdirection of Defense - and the Social Responsibilities of Computer People." *Computers and Automation*, vol. 18, no. 4, April 1969, pp. 8, 41. Editorial.

_____. "The Handwriting is on the Wall." *Computers and Automation*, vol. 20, no. 6, June 1971, p. 6. Editorial on the need for an Ombudsman.

_____. "How Do Computers Affect People?" <u>Computers</u> <u>and</u> <u>People</u>, vol. 24, no. 4, April 1975, p. 6.

_____. "Dangers from Computers, and the Social Responsibilities of Computer People." <u>Computers</u> <u>and</u> <u>People</u>, vol. 25, no. 3, March 1976, pp. 18-22.

_____. "Computers and Society: A Theme for a Course and a Final Examination." <u>Computers</u> <u>and</u> <u>People</u>, vol. 25, no. 7, July 1976, pp. 10-11.

_____. "Philosophy and Computers: Some Personal Views." <u>Computers</u> <u>and</u> <u>People</u>, vol. 26, no. 5, May 1977, pp. 16-18, 24.

_____. "Personality, Computers, and Biography." <u>Computers</u> <u>and</u> <u>People</u>, vol. 26, no. 6, June 1977, p. 6. Editorial.

_____. "Computer Misinformation from 'The New York Times.'" <u>Computers</u> <u>and</u> <u>People</u>, vol. 26, no. 7, July 1977, p. 6. Editorial.

_____. "The Nine Most Important Problems in the World, and Their Relation to Computers." <u>Computers</u> <u>and</u> <u>People</u>, vol. 28, nos. 3-4, March-April 1979, pp. 6, 10. Editorial.

Bernacchi, Richard L., and Larsen, Gerald H. <u>Data</u> <u>Processing</u> <u>Contracts</u> <u>and</u> <u>the</u> <u>Law</u>. Boston, Massachusetts: Little, Brown and Company, 1974, 715 pp.

Bernstein, Jack. <u>The</u> <u>Analytical</u> <u>Engine</u>: <u>Computers</u> - <u>Past</u>, <u>Present</u>, <u>and</u> <u>Future</u>. New York, New York: Random House, 1966.

_____. "Computers Make Lawyers' Work Easier." <u>Computers</u> <u>and</u> <u>People</u>, vol. 26, no. 5, May 1977, p. 25.

Berry, A.D. "How to Write to a Computer." <u>Retirement</u> <u>Living</u>, October 1972, pp. 26-27.

Berry, Adrian. <u>The</u> <u>Next</u> <u>Ten</u> <u>Thousand</u> <u>Years</u>: <u>A</u> <u>Vision</u> <u>of</u> <u>Man's</u> <u>Future</u> <u>in</u> <u>the</u> <u>Universe</u>. New York, New York: New American Library, 1975.

"Beyond DP: The Social Implications." <u>Datamation</u>, vol. 25, no. 8, July 1979, pp. 98-100, 102.

Biddle, A.G.W. "A Field of Clover with One Horse and Hundreds of Rabbits: The Future of the Computer and Data Processing Industries." <u>Computers</u> <u>and</u> <u>People</u>, vol. 26, no. 1, January 1977, pp. 7-9, 25, 27.

_____. "A Nut in a Nutcracker: The Small Company's Competitive Position in the EFTS Market." <u>Computers</u> <u>and</u> <u>People</u>, vol. 26, no. 2, February 1977, pp. 11-17.

_____. "The Sophisticated User is the Solution." <u>Computers</u> <u>and</u> <u>People</u>, vol. 27, no. 1, January 1978, pp. 7-9, 21, 23.

Bigelow, Robert P., ed. Computers and the Law: An Introductory Handbook. New York, New York: Commerce Clearing House, 1966.

_____. "Legal and Security Issues Posed by Computer Utilities." Harvard Business Review, vol. 45, no. 5, September-October 1967, pp. 150-152, 155-157, 160-161.

_____. "Some Legal Aspects of Commercial Remote Access Computer Services." Datamation, vol. 15, no. 8, August 1969, pp. 48-52.

_____. "What the Privacy Act of 1974 Can Mean to Computer People." Computer Law and Tax Report, April 1975, pp. 4-7.

Bigelow, Robert P., and Nycum, Susan. Your Computer and the Law. Englewood Cliffs, New Jersey: Prentice-Hall, Inc., 1975.

Bingham, H.W. "Security Techniques for EDP of Multilevel Classified Information." Griffies Air Force Base, New York: Information Processing Branch, Rome Air Development Center, Air Force Systems Command, Technical Report RADC-TR-65-415, December 1965.

Birmingham, Donald J. "Factory Data Systems Smooth Production Flow." Computer Decisions, vol. 4, no. 3, March 1972, pp. 8-13.

Bisco, Ralph L. "Social Science Data Archives: A Review of Developments." American Political Science Review, March 1966, pp. 93-109.

_____., ed. Data Bases, Computers and the Social Sciences. New York, New York: Wiley-Interscience, 1970, 291 pp.

Bitzer, Donald L.; Braunfeld, Peter G.; and Lichtenberger, W.W. "PLATO: An Automatic Teaching Device." IRE Transactions on Education, vol.5, nos. 3-4, 1961, pp. 157-161.

Bitzer, Donald L., and Johnson, R.L. "PLATO: A Computer-Based System Used in the Engineering of Education." Proceedings of the IEEE, vol. 59, no. 6, June 1971, pp. 960-968.

Blauner, Robert. Alienation and Freedom: The Factory Worker and His Industry. Chicage, Illinois: University of Chicago Press, 1964.

Block, Henry, and Ginsburg, Herbert. "The Psychology of Robots." Psychology Today, vol. 1, no. 11, April 1968, pp. 50-55.

Block, Victor. "Computer Wasteland USA." Part 1. Infosystems, vol. 24, no. 10, October 1977, pp. 40-41, 44-46. Misacquisition and misuse of computers by the federal government.

_____. "Computer Wasteland USA." Part 2. Infosystems, vol. 24, no. 11, November 1977, pp. 50-54.

Bloustein, Edward J. "Privacy as an Aspect of Human Dignity: An Answer to Dean Prosser." New York University Law Review, December 1964, pp. 962-1007.

Blum, A.M. "A General Purpose Digital Traffic Simulator."
Simulation, vol. 14, no. 1, January 1970, pp. 9-25.

Boblick, John M. "The Use of Computer-Assisted Instruction to Teach
Basic Chemical Formula Writing Skills." School Science and
Mathematics, vol. 71, no. 9, December 1971, pp. 781-789.

Bobrow, Davis B., and Schwartz, Judah L. Computers and the
Policy-Making Community: Applications to International Relations.
Englewood Cliffs, New Jersey: Prentice-Hall, Inc., 1968, 374 pp.

Bockelman, Melvin F. "The Computer: A Vital Element in Modern Day
Criminal Justice Operations." Sixth Australian Computer
Conference Proceedings, 20-24 May 1974, pp. 25-35.

_____. "Privacy and Security of Computerized Criminal Justice
Systems." Computers and Society, vol. 6, no. 1, Spring 1975, pp.
3-7.

Boeschen, John, and Currie, Sandra B. "Our Newest Computer
Teachers." Family Weekly, 6 November 1977, p. 25.

Boethe, Richard. "Hello Computers, Goodbye Privacy; Or, 1984 Is
Right Around the Corner." Cosmopolitan Magazine, vol. 166, June
1969, pp. 116-119, 170-171.

_____. "The Assault on Privacy." Newsweek, July 1970, pp. 15-20.

Boettinger, H. "Humanist Values: What Place in the Computer Age?"
Financial Executive, March 1970, pp. 44-46.

Boguslaw, Robert. The New Utopians: A Study of System Design and
Social Change." Englewood Cliffs, New Jersey: Prentice-Hall,
Inc., 1965.

Bonaldes, S.F. "A Study of the Growth of Computers in Brazil."
Poughkeepsie, New York: IBM Corporation, Technical Report
00.2748, April 1976, 35 pp.

Bone, Jan. "Turning on With CAI." American Education, vol. 10, no.
9, November 1974, pp. 33-37. Title I pupils in 32 Chicago
schools.

Boore, William F., and Murphy, G. The Computer Sampler: Management
Perspectives on the Computer. New York, New York: McGraw-Hill
Book Company, 1968.

Bord, Alfred M. "Computers in Education - the Full Spectrum."
Contemporary Education, vol. 40, no. 5, April 1969, pp. 275-279.

Borko, Harold, ed. Computer Applications in the Behavioral
Sciences. Englewood Cliffs, New Jersey: Prentice-Hall, 1962.

Borodin, A., and Gotlieb, C.C. "Computers and Employment."
Communications of the ACM, vol. 15, no. 7, July 1972, pp.
695-702.

Boruch, Robert F. "Maintaining Confidentiality of Data in Educational Research: A Systematic Analysis." *American Psychologist*, May 1971, pp. 413-430.

_____: "Stratiegies for Eliciting and Merging Confidential Social Research Data." *Policy Sciences*, September 1972, pp. 375-397.

Boulden, James B., and McLean, Ephraim R. "An Executive's Guide to Computer-Based Planning." *California Management Review*, Fall 1974, pp. 58-67.

Bournazons, Kimon, and French, Norman E. "Information Management and Privacy in Business." *Data Management*, vol. 9, no. 7, July 1971, pp. 18-23.

Boutell, Wayne S. *Auditing with the Computer*. Berkeley, California: University of California Press, 1965, 181 pp.

_____. "Auditing Through the Computer." *Journal of Accountancy*, November 1965, pp. 41-47.

_____. *Computer-Oriented Business Systems*. Englewood Cliffs, New Jersey: Prentice-Hall, Inc., 1973.

Bouvard, Marguerite Guzman, and Bouvard, Jacques. "Computerized Information and Effective Protection of Individual Rights." *Society*, September-October 1975, pp. 62-67.

Bowers, Dan M. "Computer Technology and Applications in the Next Decade." *The Office*, vol. 86, no. 1, July 1977, pp. 44, 47.

Bowles, Edmund A. *Computers in Humanistic Research: Readings and Perspectives*. Englewood Cliffs, New Jersey: Prentice-Hall, Inc., 1967, 288 pp.

_____. "Towards a Computer Curriculum for the Humanities." *Computers and the Humanities*, September 1971, pp. 35-38.

Boyle, James A. "Automated Diagnosis." *Computers and Automation*, vol. 18, no. 6, June 1969, pp. 20-22. The computer as a diagnostic aid to clinicians.

Bradbury, Ray. "Swing Low, Sweet Chariot." *Psychology Today*, vol. 2, no. 11, April 1969, pp. 43-45. Science fiction; excerpt from *The Lost City of Mars*.

Brady, Edward L., and Branscomb, Lewis M. "Information for a Changing Society." *Science*, vol. 173, 3 March 1972, pp. 961-966.

Brady, Robert A. "*Organization, Automation, and Society: The Scientific Revolution in Industry*." Berkeley, California: University of California Press, 1961.

Brady, Rodney H. "Computers in Top-Level Decision Making." *Harvard Business Review*, vol. 45, no. 4, July-August 1967, pp. 67-76.

Braibant, G. "The Individual's Right of Access to His Personal Files." Computers and People, vol. 23, no. 10, October 1974, pp. 16-20.

Braines, S.N. "A Computer Capable of Learning." Translated by A.S. Kozak. Santa Monica, California: The RAND Corporation, Report T-137, 1 March 1961, 5 pp. A Russian article that appeared in Izvestia in 1959.

Braithwaite, Timothy B. "Privacy Education for Management." Data Management, vol. 15, no. 1, January 1977, pp. 38-41.

Brand, S. "Spacewar: Fanatic Life and Symbolic Death Among the Computer Bums." Rolling Stone, no. 123, 7 December 1972, pp. 50-58.

Brand, Stewart. Two Cybernetic Frontiers. New York, New York: Random House, 1974.

Brandin, David. "Public Policy on Privacy." Computers and Society, Spring 1976, pp. 14-18.

Brandt, Richard B. Ethical Theory. Englewood Cliffs, New Jersey: Prentice-Hall, Inc., 1959.

Branscomb, Lewis M. "Future Computer." Across the Board, vol. 16, no. 3, March 1979, pp. 61-68.

Branstan, Dennis K. "Privacy and Protection in Operating Systems." Computer, vol. 6, no. 1, January 1973, pp. 43-46. Workshop report from the IEEE Committee on Operating Systems.

Braun, Ludwig. "Magic for Educators: Microcomputers." Personal Computing, vol. 2, no. 1, January 1978, pp. 30-38, 40.

Braunfeld, Peter G. "Problems and Prospects of Teaching with a Computer." Journal of Educational Psychology, vol. 55, no. 4, 1964, pp. 201-211. Computer-based PLATO II system.

Braunfeld, Peter G., and Fosdick, L.D. "The Use of an Automatic Computer System in Teaching." IRE Transactions on Education, vol. 4, no. 4, 1962, pp. 156-167.

Bray, Melvyn. "How Safe Is Your System?" Data Systems, December 1971, pp. 12-15. Computer threats and appropriate countermeasures.

Brenner, Steven N., and Molander, Earl A. "Is the Ethics of Business Changing?" Harvard Business Review, vol. 55, no. 1, January-February 1977, pp. 57-71.

Brewer, Garry D. Politicians, Bureaucrats, and the Consultant: A Critique of Urban Problem Solving. New York, New York: Basic Books, 1973.

Brickman, W.W., and Lehner, S. Automation, Education and Human Values. New York, New York: School and Society Books, 1966.

Brictson, R.C. "Some Thoughts on the Social Implications of Computers and Privacy." Santa Monica, California: System Development Corporation, Report SP-2953, 14 March 1968.

Bride, Edward J. "Insurance May Be Cheaper Than Security." Computerworld, 6 September 1972, p. 3.

Briggs, Leslie J. "The Probable Role of Teaching Machines in Classroom Practice." Theory into Practice, vol. 1, 1962, pp. 47-56.

Britton, Keith. "The Home Computer." In Digest of Papers, pp. 218-219. New York, New York: The Institute of Electrical and Electronics Engineers, Inc., Spring COMPCON76, IEEE Catalog No. 76CH1069-4(CR), February 1976.

Brix, V.H. Are You a Computer: Cybernetics in Everyday Life. New York, New York: Emerson Books, 1967.

Broad, Charlie Dunbar. Five Types of Ethical Theory. New York, New York: Humanities Press, 1962.

Brock, Gerald W. The United States Computer Industry: A Study of Market Power. Cambridge, Massachusetts: Ballinger Publishing Company, 1975.

Brockett, Donald C., and McClain, Malcolm E. "Case-Tracking/Evaluation System for Law Office." Journal of Systems Management, August 1975, pp. 38-44.

Brodey, W.M., and Lindren, N. "Human Enhancement: Beyond the Machine Age." IEEE Spectrum, February 1968, pp. 79-93.

Bronowski, J. Science and Human Values. New York, New York: Harper and Row, 1965.

Bronwell, Arthur B., ed. Science and Technology in the World of the Future. New York, New York: John Wiley and Sons, 1970, 395 pp.

Brooks, Harvey. "Technology and Values: New Ethical Issues Raised by Technological Progress." Zygon, March 1973, pp. 17-35.

Brooks, Jack. "Data About People Can Be Used for Good or Evil." Computers and People, vol. 23, no. 1, January 1974, pp. 31-32.

Broudy, H.S. "Science, Technology, and the Diminished Mind." Journal of College Science Teaching, May 1976, pp. 292-296.

Brown, Arthur W. "Professionalism--Let's Give It a New Dimension." San Jose, California: IBM Corporation, Technical Note 02.075, 5 November 1974, 15 pp.

Brown, Dean. "On Computers and Learning." Computer Decisions, vol. 6, no. 5, May 1974, pp. 41-42.

Brown, Dean, and Cole, Phyllis M. "The Classroom Microcomputer." Computer Decisions, vol. 7, no. 2, February 1975, pp. 34-35.

Brown, Dean, and El-Ghannam, Mohammed A. "Computers for Teaching." *Computer*, vol. 6, no. 1, January 1973, pp. 16-22.

Brown, J.A. *Computers and Automation*. New York, New York: Arco Publishing Company, 1968.

Brown, L., and Marks, S. *Electric Media*. New York, New York: Harcourt Brace Jovanovich, 1974.

Brown, Martin, ed. *The Social Responsibility of the Scientist*. New York, New York: The Free Press, 1971, 282 pp.

Browne, Peter S. "Computer Security - A Survey." *AFIPS Conference Proceedings*, vol. 45, 7-10 June 1976, pp. 53-63.

Brudner, Harvey J. "Computer-Managed Instrution." *Science*, vol. 162, no. 3857, 29 November 1968, pp. 970-976.

Bruk, I. "Electronic Computers in the Service of the National Economy." Translated by John Olney. Santa Monica, California: The RAND Corporation, Report T-135, 12 January 1961, 11 pp. A Russian article that appeared in *Kommunist* in 1957.

Bruno, Jim N. "Privacy: An Issue For the Eighties." *Administrative Management*, vol. 40, no. 8, August 1979, pp. 33-35, 68.

Bruns, Becky. "A Computer of Your Own." *Dixie*, 2 October 1977, pp. 6-8, 42-45.

Bryan, Glenn L. "Computers and Education." *Computers and Automation*, vol. 18, no. 3, March 1969, pp. 16-19.

Brzezinski, Zbigniew. "The American Transition." *New Republic*, 23 December 1967, pp. 18-21.

Buckley, J.L. "The Future of Computers in Security and Law Enforcement." Part 1. *Law and Order*, August 1965, pp. 36-38.

_____. "The Future of Computers in Security and Law Enforcement." Part 2. *Law and Order*, September 1965, pp. 48-50, 52.

Bueschel, R.T. "Time Sharing in the Near Future." *Computers and Automation*, vol. 18, no. 1, January 1969, pp. 28-30.

Bunnell, David. *Personal Computing: A Beginner's Guide*. New York, New York: Hawthorn Books, Inc., 1978.

Burck, Gilbert H. "Knowledge: The Biggest Growth Industry of Them All." *Fortune*, November 1964, pp. 128-131, 267-268, 270.

Burck, Gilbert H., and the editors of *Fortune*. *The Computer Age and its Potential for Management*. New York, New York: Harper and Row, 1965.

Burke, Edmund L. "Discovering Illicit Computer Usage." In _Digest of Papers_, pp. 178-180. New York, New York: The Institute of Electrical and Electronics Engineers, Inc., Spring COMPCON76, IEEE Catalog No. 76CH1069-4(CR), February 1976.

Burke, John G., ed. _The New Technology and Human Values_. Belmont, California: Wadsworth, 1966.

_____. "Technology and Values." In _The Great Ideas Today 1969_, pp. 190-215. Chicago, Illinois: Encyclopaedia Britannica, Inc., 1969.

Burkett, Leonard, and Norfleet, Morris. "CAI in Eastern Kentucky." _Contempory Education_, vol. 40, no. 5, April 1969, pp. 290-292.

Burlingame, J.F. "Information Technology and Decentralization." _Harvard Business Review_, vol. 39, no. 6, November-December 1961, pp. 121-126.

Burns, J., and Peltason, J. _Government by the People_. Englewood Cliffs, New Jersey: Prentice-Hall, Inc., 1964.

Burstyn, H. Paris. "Electronic Fund Transfers: A Promise or a Threat?" _Personal Computing_, vol. 2, no. 5, May 1978, pp. 58, 60-63, 66.

Burton, Dolores Marie. "Some Uses of a Grammatical Concordance." _Computers and the Humanities_, vol. 2, no. 4, March 1968, pp. 145-154.

Burton, Ellison S., ed. _Computers and Operations Research: Environmental Applications_. Elmsford, New York: Pergamon Press, Inc., 1977.

Bush, Vannevar. _Science Is Not Enough: Reflections for the Present and Future_. New York, New York: William Morrow, 1967, 192 pp.

Bushnell, Don D., and Allen, Dwight W., eds. _The Computer in American Education_. New York, New York: John Wiley and Sons, 1967.

Butel, Jane. "Consumer Protection and Electronic Funds Transfer." _Computers and People_, vol. 27, no. 1, January 1978, pp. 10-11, 21, 23.

Butler, David. "Impact of Computers on the Industrial Power Structure." _Computer Bulletin_, vol. 13, no. 10, October 1969, pp. 344-347.

Button, C., and Janasiewicz, C. "Data-Base Administration in a Manufacturing Environment: A Genesis." Poughkeepsie, New York: IBM Corporation, Technical Report 00.2801, February 1977, 17 pp.

Byrne, Dan R., Jr., and Scott, George M. "Closing the Computer Audit Gap." _Internal Auditor_, vol. 34, no. 2, April 1977, pp. 27-32.

Cain, J.T. "Microprocessors and Education." *Computer*, vol. 10, January 1977, pp. 9-10.

Calder, Nigel. "Brains Versus Computers: How Much Decision-Making Can We Leave to the Machine?" *New Statesman*, 17 May 1968, pp. 645-648.

_____. *Technopolis: Social Control of the Uses of Science*. New York, New York: Simon and Schuster, 1970.

Callahan, Daniel J. *The Tyranny of Survival: On a Science of Technology Limits*. New York, New York: The Macmillan Company, 1973.

_____. "Science: Limits and Prohibitions. *Hastings Center Report*, November 1973, pp. 5-7.

_____. "Science and Ethics." *American Scholar*, Summer 1975, pp. 439-456. From *The Nature of Scientific Discovery*.

_____. "Scientists and Humanists." *Hastings Center Report*, June 1976, pp. 20, 34.

Campaigne, Howard, and Hoffman, Lance J. "Computer Privacy and Security." *Computers and Automation*, vol. 22, no. 7, July 1973, pp. 12-17.

Campbell, Angus, and Converse, Phillip E., eds. *The Human Meaning of Social Change*." New York, New York: Russell Sage Foundation, 1972.

Campbell, Voin R. "Privacy and Security in Local Government Infosystems." *Infosystems*, December 1976, pp. 31, 34.

"Can Systems Analysis Solve Social Problems?" *Datamation*, vol. 20, no. 6, June 1974, pp. 82-83, 86-87, 91-92.

Canning, Richard G., ed. "The Question of Professionalism." *EDP Analyzer*, vol. 6, no. 12, December 1968, 13 pp.

_____., ed. "Long-Term Retention of Data." *EDP Analyzer*, vol. 11, no. 7, July 1973.

_____., ed. "The Debate on Information Privacy: Part 1." *EDP Analyzer*, vol. 13, no. 11, November 1975.

_____., ed. "The Debate on Information Privacy: Part 2." *EDP Analyzer*, vol. 13, no. 12, December 1975.

_____., ed. "Integrity and Security of Personal Data." *EDP Analyzer*, vol. 14, no. 4, April 1976.

_____., ed. "Word Processing: Part 1." *EDP Analyzer*, vol. 15, no. 2, February 1977, 12 pp.

_____., ed. "Word Processing: Part 2." *EDP Analyzer*, vol. 15, no. 3, March 1977, 14 pp.

_____., ed. "Computer Message Systems." <u>EDP Analyzer</u>, vol. 15, no. 4, April 1977.

Canning, Richard G., and Sisson, Roger L. <u>The Management of Data Processing</u>. New York, New York: John Wiley and Company, 1967.

Carey, James W., and Quirk, John J. "The Mythos of the Electronic Revolution." Part 1. <u>American Scholar</u>, vol. 39, no. 2, Spring 1970, pp. 219-241.

_____. "The Mythos of the Electronic Revolution." Part 2. <u>American Scholar</u>, vol. 39, no. 3, Summer 1970, pp. 395-424.

Carlson, Eric D. "Decision Support Systems: Personal Computing Services for Managers." <u>Management Review</u>, vol. 66, no. 1, January 1977, pp. 4-11.

Carlson, Walter M. "A Management Information System Designed by Managers." <u>Datamation</u>, vol. 13, no. 5, May 1967, pp. 37-43.

Carney, P.L. "Police Say Mafia's DP Use Impedes Crime Prevention." <u>Computerworld</u>, 2 December 1970, p. 1.

_____. "'Suspected Companies' on Crime Commission Lists." <u>Computerworld</u>, 30 December 1970, p. 1. Mafia connected businesses that use computers.

Carr, W.A. "Home Terminals: Some Educational Considerations." Kingston, New York: IBM Corporation, Technical Report 21.498, September 1972, 9 pp.

Carroll, John M. "How Safe Is Your Computer?" <u>Business Quarterly</u>, Autumn 1971, pp. 86-89.

_____. <u>Computer Security</u>. Los Angeles, California: Security World Publishing Company, Inc., 1977.

Cary, Frank T. "Computer Changes Management Art." <u>Iron Age</u>, vol. 195, 7 January 1964, pp. 164-166.

_____., an interview with. "IBM's Guidelines to Employee Privacy." <u>Harvard Business Review</u>, vol. 54, no. 5, September-October 1976, pp. 82-90.

Cashman, T.J. "How the Data Processing Industry has Failed Education." <u>AFIPS Conference Proceedings</u>, vol. 43, 6-10 May 1974, pp. 231-233.

Casper, G. Gary. "Why Certification?" <u>Infosystems</u>, vol. 24, no. 7, July 1977, p. 81.

Cassey, Douglas A. <u>Introduction to Computer-Aided Manufacturing in Electronics</u>. New York, New York: John Wiley and Sons, 1972, 248 pp.

CBEMA. "The Role of Computers in...Privacy, Confidentiality, Data Security." Washington, D.C.: 1973, 12 pp.

_____. "Government Looks at Privacy and Security in Computer Systems: A Speech by Dr. Ruth M. Davis." Washington, D.C.: 1974, 21 pp.

_____. "Privacy Legislation." Washington, D.C.: 1974, 61 pp.

_____. "Privacy: The Private Sector and Society's Needs." Washington, D.C.: 1975, 15 pp. Text of address given by Willis H. Ware before a meeting of Share, Inc. held 5 March 1975.

_____. "Information Technology and Individual Privacy." Washington, D.C.: 1975, 37 pp. Transcript of formal portion of symposium at the 141st American Association for the Advancement of Science meeting held 27 January 1975.

_____. "Privacy: A Challenge to Corporate Leadership." Washington, D.C.: 1976, 8 pp.

_____. "Privacy Issues and the Private Sector." Washington, D.C.: 1976, 10 pp.

Cerf, Vinton G., and Curran, Alex. "The Future of Computer Communications." *Datamation*, vol. 23, no. 5, May 1977, pp. 105-108, 112, 114.

Chain, E. *Social Responsibility and the Scientist in Modern Western Society*. London, England: The Council of Christians and Jews, 1970.

Chambers, A.D. "Computer Fraud and Abuse." *The Computer Journal*, vol. 21, no. 3, August 1978, pp. 194-197.

Chamis, Alice Yanosko. "The Design of Information Systems." *Law and Computer Technology*, September 1969, pp. 2-14.

Chanana, Charanjit. *Computers in Asia*. New York, New York: International Publishing Service, 1974.

Chant, Verne G., and others. "World Models: Utility or Futility." *Optimum*, vol. 7, no. 3, 1976, pp. 5-21.

Charp, Sylvia. "A Computer-Assisted Instruction System." *Audio-Visual Instruction*, vol. 14, no. 3, March 1969, pp. 61-62.

Chartrand, Robert L. *Systems Technology Applied to Social and Community Problems*. New York, New York: Spartan Books, 1971.

_____. *Computers and Political Campaigning*. New York, New York: Spartan Books, 1972

_____., ed. *Computers in the Service of Society*. Elmsford, New York: Pergamon Press, Inc., 1972.

Cheng, V.; Eberlein, S.; and Donahue, S. "Computer's Potential in Society." *Data Management*, vol. 9, no. 8, August 1971, pp. 40-43.

Chepark, Robert. "A Decade of Challenges Awaits 'Electro-Banking.'" *Data Management*, vol. 15, no. 3, March 1977, pp. 24-26.

Chirlian, Paul M. *Understanding Computers*. Forest Grove, Oregon: International Scholarly Book Service, Inc., 1978.

Chu, Albert L.C. "Computer Security: The Corporate Achilles Heel." *Business Administration*, 1 February 1971, pp. 32-38.

_____. "The Need to Know - The Right to Privacy." *Business Automation*, June 1971, pp. 31-35.

Clark, David D., and Redell, David D. *Protection of Information in Computer Systems*. Long Beach, California: IEEE Computer Society, Catalog No. 75CH1050-4, 1975, 260 pp. Tutorial.

Clark, Henry. "When the 'UPC' Symbol Takes Over Completely." *MAD Magazine*, no. 198, April 1978, pp. 14-16.

Clark, Lawrence M. "Putting Common Sense into Computers: What is Common Sense?" *Computers and People*, vol. 26, no. 5, May 1977, pp. 19-23.

_____. "Putting Common Sense into Computers: Designing a Computer Program so as to Have Common Sense." Part 1. *Computers and People*, vol. 26, no. 6, June 1977, pp. 17-22.

_____. "Putting Common Sense into Computers: Designing a Computer Program so as to Have Common Sense." Part 2. *Computers and People*, vol. 26, no. 7, July 1977, pp. 18-21.

_____. "Putting Common Sense into Computers: Some Principles of Design." *Computers and People*, vol. 27, no. 4, April 1978, pp. 13-17.

Clarke, Arthur C. *Profiles of the Future*. New York, New York: Harper and Row, Publishers, 1958.

_____. *2001: A Space Odyssey*. New York, New York: New American Library, 1968. Science fiction.

_____. "The Mind of the Machine." *Playboy*, December 1968, pp. 116-119, 122, 293-294.

_____. "Are You Thinking Machines?" *Industrial Research*, vol. 11, March 1969, pp. 52-55.

Clubb, Jerome M., and Allen, Howard. "Computers and Historical Studies." *Journal of American History*, December 1967, pp. 599-607.

Clubb, Jerome M., and Traugott, Michael W. *Using Computers*. Washington, D.C.: American Political Science Association, 1978.

Clutterbuck, David. "Turning the Key on Employees' Personal Records." *International Management*, vol. 33, no. 12, December 1978, pp. 44-47.

Coan, David R.A. "Code of Practice - A Call for Comment." *Computer Bulletin*, December 1976, pp. 4-5.

"Code of Conduct Arises from AFIPS Workshop." *Computerworld*, vol. 12, no. 36, 4 September 1978, pp. 12, 16.

Cohen, K.J., and Rhenman, E. "The Role of Management Games in Education and Research." *Management Science*, vol. 7, January 1961, pp. 131-166.

Cohen, R.E. "Agencies Prepare Regulations for Implementing New Privacy Laws." *National Journal Reports*, vol. 7, 24 May 1975, pp. 774-777.

Colbert, Douglas A. *Computers and Management for Business*. New York, New York: Van Nostrand Reinhold Company, 1975.

Colby, K.M.; Watt, J.B.; and Gilbert, J.P. "A Computer Method of Psychotherapy: Preliminary Communication." *The Journal of Nervous and Mental Disease*, vol. 142, no. 2, 1966, pp. 148-152.

Collen, Morris F., ed. *Hospital Computer Systems*. New York, New York: John Wiley and Sons, 1974, 768 pp.

Colstad, Ken, and Lipkin, Efrem. "Community Memory: A Public Information Network." In *Computer Technology to Reach the People: Digest of Papers*, pp. 199-201. New York, New York: The Institute of Electrical and Electronics Engineers, Inc., Spring COMPCON75, IEEE Catalog No. 75CH0920-9C, February 1975. Also in *Computers and Society*, Winter 1975, pp. 6-7.

Colton, Kent W. "Computers and Police: Patterns of Success and Failure." *Computers and Society*, Winter 1973, pp. 4-13. Also in *Sloan Management Review*, vol. 14, no. 2, Winter 1973, pp. 75-97.

Comarow, Avery. "When Conscience and Career Collide." *Money*, September 1976, pp. 48-50, 52, 54.

Communication Breakthrough in the Fight Against Crime: National Crime Information Center. Washington, D.C.: Federal Bureau of Investigation, 1970, 20 pp.

"Computer-Based Justice Identification and Intelligence System." *Digital Computer Newsletter*, April 1965, pp. 52-53.

"Computer Maintained Health Records Offer More Privacy than Manual Files." *Minicomputer News*, vol. 3, no. 4, 24 February 1977, p. 2.

"Computer People Must Protect Society from Our Wrongdoings." *CIPS Computer Magazine*, May 1974, pp. 13-14.

Computer Privacy. United States Senate, Subcommittee on Administrative Practice and Procedure, Committee on the Judiciary, 90th Congress, 1st Session, 14-15 March 1967.

"Computer Privacy." Scientific American, vol. 236, no. 2, February 1977, p. 50.

"Computer Technology May Take Us Back to Cottage Industries." CIPS Computer Magazine, January 1974, pp. 10-11, 18.

"Computer Threats!" Scottsdale, Arizona: Motorola, Inc., 1977, 10 pp.

"Computerized Cars." Scientific American, vol. 233, no. 2, August 1975, p. 48.

"Computerized Grocery Checkouts." Better Homes and Gardens, February 1976, p. 111.

"Computers and Communications: A Future of Nightmares or Pleasant Dreams." Saving and Loan News, vol. 97, no. 12, December 1976, pp. 58-61.

"Computers and Some Moral Questions - Roundup 1." Computers and Automation, vol. 16, no. 7, July 1967, pp. 28-29, 32-35.

"Computers and Some Moral Questions - Roundup 2." Computers and Automation, vol. 16, no. 9, September 1967, pp. 10-11.

"Computers and Some Moral Questions - Roundup 3." Computers and Automation, vol. 16, no. 11, November 1967, pp. 10-12.

"Computers in Handling - The Three Major Areas of Application." Modern Materials Handling, vol. 32, no. 1, January 1977, pp. 72-80.

"Computers that Write You Personal Notes from Capital Hill." U.S. News and World Report, vol. 85, 16 October 1978, pp. 47-48.

Conklin, G., ed. Science-Fiction Thinking Machines: Robots, Androids, Computers. New York, New York: Vanguard Press, Inc., 1954.

Connally, G.E. "Personnel Administration and the Computer." Personnel Journal, vol. 48, August 1969, pp. 605-611.

Connolly, John A. "Using Computers to Individualize Instruction: Another Approach." Computers and Automation, vol. 20, no. 3, March 1971, pp. 8-13.

Cook, Nathan H. "Computer-Managed Parts Manufacuture." Scientific American, vol. 232, no. 2, February 1975, pp. 22-29.

Cooley, Mike. "Computers, Automation and Technological Change." Computers and Automation, vol. 22, no. 3, March 1973, pp. 15-17, 25.

Cooley, William W. "Computer Assistance for Individualized Education." Journal of Educational Data Processing, vol. 7, no. 1, February 1970, pp. 18-21.

Cooley, William W., and Glaser, Robert. "The Computer and Individualized Instruction." *Science*, vol. 166, no. 3905, October 1969, pp. 574-582.

Coon, Thomas F. "Technological Law Enforcement - Victory and Voids." *Police*, January-February 1968, pp. 19-22.

Cosby, H. Douglas. "Secrecy vs. Confidentiality." *Data Management*, vol. 12, no. 1, January 1974, pp. 20-21.

"Cost, Codes, People and the Constitution." *Datamation*, vol. 22, no. 5, May 1976, pp. 180-182.

Cottle, Thomas J. "Our Soul-Baring Orgy Destroys the Private Self." *Psychology Today*, October 1975, pp. 22-23, 87.

Couger, J. Daniel, ed. "Books Useful in Teaching Business Applications of the Computer." 10th edition. *Computing Newsletter*, vol. 10, no. 5, January 1977, 22 pp.

Couger, J. Daniel, and McFadden, Fred R. *Introduction to Computer-Based Information Systems*. New York, New York: John Wiley and Sons, 1975.

Couger, J. Daniel, and Zawacki, Robert A. "What Motivates DP Professionals." *Datamation*, vol. 24, no. 9, September 1978, pp. 116-123.

Coulson, John E., and others. "Effects of Branching in a Computer Controlled Autoinstruction Device." *Journal of Applied Psychology*, vol. 46, no. 6, 1962, pp. 389-392.

Coulson, John E., and Silberman, Harry F. "Effects of Three Variables in a Teaching Machine." *Journal of Educational Psychology*, vol. 51, no. 3, June 1960, pp. 135-143.

——. "Automated Teaching and Individual Differences." *Audiovisual Communication Review*, vol. 9, 1961, pp. 5-15.

Countryman, Vern. "Computers and Dossiers - Part 1." *Computers and Automation*, vol. 21, no. 1, January 1972, pp. 13-19, 42.

——. "Computers and Dossiers - Part 2." *Computers and Automation*, vol. 21, no. 2, February 1972, pp. 14-20, 36.

Courtney, Robert H., Jr. "Data Security - An IBM Overview." Poughkeepsie, New York: IBM Corporation, December 1973.

——. "Security Risk Assessment in Electronic Data Processing Systems." Poughkeepsie, New York: IBM Corporation, December 1975.

Cowden, Peter, and Cowden, Christin. "Certification: A Bogus Solution." *Infosystems*, vol. 24, no. 11, November 1977, p. 65.

Cox, Edwin B., and Giese, Paul E. "Now It's the 'Less-Check Society.'" *Harvard Business Review*, vol. 50, no. 6, November-December 1972, pp. 6-8, 10, 12, 16, 18, 148-149.

Craig, John. "Car Pooling and Personal Computers." *Creative Computing*, vol. 5, no. 11, November 1979, pp. 74-82.

Crecine, John P. "Computer Simulation in Urban Research." *Public Administration Review*, January-February 1968, pp. 66-77.

Cressey, D.R. *Other People's Money: The Social Psychology of Embezzlement*. New York, New York: The Free Press, 1953.

Crichton, Michael. *The Terminal Man*. New York, New York: Alfred A. Knopf, Inc., 1972. Science fiction.

Croisdale, D.W. "Data Processing Professionalism: A Must or a Myth." *Management Services in Government*, vol. 32, no. 3, August 1977, pp. 151-157.

Crosby, Jack L. *Computer Simulation in Genetics*. New York, New York: John Wiley and Sons, 1973, 477 pp.

Cross, James S. "I, You, We...Elements of a Computer Environment." *Infosystems*, August 1975, p. 49.

Crowder, Norman A. "On the Differences Between Linear and Intrinsic Programing." *Phi Delta Kappan*, vol. 44, March 1963, pp. 250-254. Programmed learning.

Crowley, Thomas H. *Understanding Computers*. New York, New York: McGraw-Hill Book Company, 1967, 139 pp.

Culbertson, J.T. *The Minds of Robots*. Urbana, Illinois: University of Illinois Press, 1963.

Cullen, Mike, and Assemblyman, C.A. "Fear of Business Computer Abuse Must Be Calmed by Privacy Laws." *Data Management*, vol. 15, no. 4, April 1977, pp. 18-20.

Cummings, Joan Greenbaum. "Automation and Unemployment: A Look at the Basic Assumptions in the Computer Field." *Computers and Society*, Fall 1975, pp. 4-5.

Cunliffe, Marcus. "The American Way - Private Property." *The Center Magazine*, September-October 1976, pp. 16-21.

Curran, William J., and others. "Protection of Privacy and Confidentiality." *Science*, 23 November 1973, pp. 797-802.

Dalkey, N., ed. *Studies in the Quality of Life: Delphi and Decisionmaking*. Lexington, Massachusetts: D.C. Health and Company, 1972.

Dansiger, Sheldon J. "Embezzling Primer." Computers and Automation, vol. 16, no. 11, November 1967, pp. 41-43.

Danziger, James N. "Computer Technology and the Local Budgetary System." Southern Review of Public Administration, vol. 1, no. 3, December 1977, pp. 279-292.

Darby, Ralph L. "Information Analysis Centers as a Source for Information and Data." Special Libraries, February 1968, pp. 91-97.

Data Processing Management in the Federal Government. United States House of Representatives, Subcommittee on Government Activities, Committee on Government Operations, 90th Congress, 1st Session, 18-20 July 1967.

David, E.E., Jr., and Fano, Robert M. "Some Thoughts About Social Implications of Accessible Computing." AFIPS Conference Proceedings, FJCC, vol. 27, Part 1, November-December 1965, pp. 243-247.

David, Heather M. "Computers, Privacy, and Security." Computer Decisions, vol. 6, no. 2, February 1974, pp. 28-30.

Davidson, Daniel M. "Quality Control in a Computer Data Utility." Computers and People, vol. 26, no. 4, April 1977, pp. 11-12, 26.

Davidson, Timothy A. "Computer Information Privacy." The Office, vol. 70, no. 2, August 1969, pp. 10-17.

Davis, Gordon B. Management Information Systems: Conceptual Foundations, Structure, and Development. New York, New York: McGraw-Hill Book Company, 1974.

Davis, K.C. "The Information Act: A Preliminary Analysis." University of Chicago Law Review, vol. 34, 1967, pp. 761-812.

Davis, N.C., and Goodman, S.E. "The Soviet Bloc's Unified System of Computers." Computing Surveys, vol. 10, no. 2, June 1978, pp. 93-122.

Davis, Robert H. "The Computer Revolution and the Spirit of Man." AFIPS Conference Proceedings, SJCC, vol. 25, 21-23 April 1964, pp. 161-167.

Davis, Ruth M. "Privacy and Security in Data Systems." Computers and People, vol. 23, no. 3, March 1974, pp. 20-27.

_____. "Impermanent Balance between Man and Computer." Science, 11 October 1974, p. 99. Editorial.

_____. "The Computer Serves, the Consumer Relishes." Computer Decisions, vol. 7, no. 5, May 1975, pp. 31-34.

_____. "The Data Encryption Standard in Perspective." Communications, vol. 16, no. 6, November 1978, pp. 5-9.

Dawson, Edward H. "Just Another Tool? CAI." _Audiovisual Instruction_, vol. 15, no. 6, June-July 1970, pp. 92-93.

Dean, Neal J. "The Computer Comes of Age." _Harvard Business Review_, vol. 46, no. 1, January-February 1968, pp. 83-91.

Dearden, John. "Myth of Real-Time Management Information." _Harvard Business Review_, vol. 44, no. 3, May-June 1966, pp. 123-132.

_____. "MIS is a Mirage." _Harvard Business Review_, vol. 50, no. 1, January-February 1972, pp. 90-99.

"Debate Will Rage and Confuse the Issues, but a National Data Center will Become Reality." _Business Automation_, January 1970, pp. 62-63.

de Bono, E. _The Mechanism of Mind_. New York, New York: Simon and Schuster, 1969.

Dechert, Charles R., ed. _The Social Impact of Cybernetics_. New York, New York: Simon and Schuster, 1967.

Deep, Donald. "The Computer Can Help Individualize Instruction." _Elementary School Journal_, vol. 40, no. 7, April 1970, pp. 351-358.

de Gennaro, Richard. "The Development and Administration of Automated Systems in Academic Libraries." _Journal of Library Automation_, vol. 1, March 1968, pp. 75-91.

_____. "Automation in the Harvard College Library." _Harvard Library Bulletin_, vol. 16, July 1968, pp. 217-236.

de George, Richard T., ed. _Ethics and Society: Original Essays on Contempory Moral Problems_. New York, New York: Doubleday and Company, 1966.

de Grazia, Sebastian. _Of Time, Work and Leisure_. New York, New York: The Twentieth Century Fund, 1962.

Delatte, Louis. "Computers and the Classics: A Supplement." _Computers and the Humanities_, vol. 2, no. 3, January 1968, pp. 117-120.

Demczynski, S. _Automation and the Future of Man_. London, England: George Allen and Unwin, Ltd., 1964.

Dennis, R.L. "Security in the Computer Environment." Santa Monica, California: System Development Corporation, Report SP 2440/000/01, 18 August 1966.

Dent, Ike. "Legislation Proposed Against Computer Fraud." _Credit World_, vol. 66, no. 5, February 1978, p. 11.

de Rossi, Claude J. _Computers: Tools for Today_. Chicago, Illinois: Children's Press, 1972.

Devey, D.P. "The Managing of Employee Personal Information." In *Proceedings of Share 50*, pp. 1371-1385. Chicago, Illinois: Share Inc., March 1978.

Devlin, Gerald W. "EDP Security Control." *The Internal Auditor*, July-August 1974, pp. 16-25.

de Vos, Marina; Kessis, Jean-Jacques; and Robyn, Rose. "Developments in Computer-Assisted Instruction in France." *Educational Technology*, vol. 11, no. 8, August 1971, pp. 47-49.

DeWeese, J. Taylor. "Giving the Computer a Conscience." *Harper's*, vol. 247, no. 1482, November 1973, pp. 14, 16-17.

_____. "The Trojan Horse Caper - and Assorted Other Computer Crimes." *Saturday Review*, 15 November 1975, pp. 10, 58-60.

Dewhurst, J. Frederick. *America's Needs and Resources: A New Survey*. New York, New York: The Twentieth Century Fund, 1955.

Dick, Walter; Latta, Raymond; and Rivers, Leroy. "Sources of Information on Computer-Assisted Instruction." *Educational Technology*, vol. 10, no. 3, March 1970, pp. 36-38.

Dickey, C. Lewis. "Securing the Computer." *Journal of Systems Management*, February 1972, pp. 8-10.

Didday, Richard. *Home Computers: 201 Questions and Answers, Volume 1, Hardware*. Forest Grove, Oregon: International Scholarly Book Services, Inc., 1977.

_____. *Home Computers: 201 Questions and Answers, Volume 2, Software*. Forest Grove, Oregon: International Scholarly Book Services, Inc., 1977.

Diebold, John. *Automation*. New York, New York: Van Nostrand, 1952.

_____. *Beyond Automation*. New York, New York: McGraw-Hill Book Company, 1964.

_____. "Computers, Program Management, and Foreign Affairs." *Foreign Affairs*, October 1966, pp. 125-134.

_____. "What's Ahead for Computer Technology?" *Management Review*, December 1967, pp. 28-31.

_____. *Man and the Computer: Technology as an Agent of Social Change*. New York, New York: Frederick A. Praeger, Publishers, 1969, 157 pp.

_____. "Bad Decisions on Computer Use." *Harvard Business Review*, vol. 47, no. 1, January-February 1969, pp. 14-16, 27-28, 176.

_____., ed. *The World of the Computer*. New York, New York: Random House, 1973.

_____., an interview with. "What People Have to Do to Keep Up with Machines." U.S. News and World Report, 19 January 1973, pp. 42-44.

Distefano, Stephen. "The DP Manager and the Corporate Organization." Data Processing, vol. 14, 1970, pp. 275-279.

Dolby, J.L.; Forsyth, V.J.; and Resnikoff, H.L. Computerized Library Catalogues: Their Growth, Cost and Utility. Cambridge, Massachusetts: MIT Press, 1969.

Dolotta, Ted A. Data Processing in 1980-1985: A Study of Potential Limitations to Progress. New York, New York: John Wiley and Sons, 1976.

Dolotta, Ted A., and others. "Data Processing in 1980-1985." New York, New York: Share, Inc., SSD No. 249, 15 October 1974, 61 pp.

Donnelly, Caroline. "A Free-Spending, Job-Squeezed, House-Proud Future." Money, May 1976, pp. 96-98, 100.

Dorf, Richard C. Computers and Man. San Francisco, California: Boyd-Fraser Publishing, 1974, 469 pp.

Douglas, A.S. "The U.K. Privacy White Paper 1975." AFIPS Conference Proceedings, vol. 45, 7-10 June 1976, pp. 33-38.

Douglas, J. The Technological Threat. Englewood Cliffs, New Jersey: Prentice-Hall, Inc., 1971.

Dowling, R. "Congress Urged to Enact Access Curbs Before EFT Development." American Banker, vol. 141, no. 209, 27 October 1976, pp. 1, 24.

Dozier, Gary W. "A Plentiful Harvest." Personal Computing, vol. 2, no. 4, April 1978, pp. 57-70. A microcomputer gardening application.

"DP in Government is Shockingly Mismanaged, Study Shows." Administrative Management, vol. 39, no. 9, September 1978, pp. 26-27, 102. "Old equipment, weak management, and confused policy."

Drazen, Erica, and others. "Requirements for Computerized Patient Monitoring Systems." Computer, January 1975, pp. 22-26.

Dreyfus, Hubert L. What Computers Can't Do: A Critique of Artificial Reason. New York, New York: Harper and Row, 1972, 259 pp.

_____. "Artificial Intelligence." The Annals of the American Academy of Politcal and Social Science, vol. 412, March 1974, pp. 21-33.

Drozda, Thomas J. "Manufacturing Control: Is Your Company Ready for the Impact of Computers." Production, vol. 82, no. 6, December 1978, pp. 50-57.

Drucker, Peter F. The Age of Discontinuity: Guidelines to Our Changing Society. New York, New York: Harper and Row, 1969.

Duggan, Michael A. "Law, Logic, and the Computer: Bibliography with Assorted Background Material." Computing Reviews, vol. 7, no. 1, January-February 1966, pp. 95-117.

_____. "Computer Utilities - Social and Policy Implications: A Reference Bibliography." Computing Reviews, vol. 9, no. 10, October 1968, pp. 631-647.

Dunlop, John T., ed. Automation and Technological Change. Englewood Cliffs, New Jersey: Prentice-Hall, Inc., 1962.

Dunn, Alex, and Wastler, Jean. Computer-Assisted Instruction, Final Report. Rockville, Maryland: Montgomery County Public Schools, 1972, 507 pp.

Dunn, Edger S., Jr. "The Idea of a National Data Center and the Issue of Personal Privacy." The American Statistician, vol. 21, no. 1, February 1967, pp. 21-27.

Dunn, Nina. "The Office of the Future - Part 1." Computer Decisions, vol. 11, no. 7, July 1979, pp. 16-19, 23, 26.

_____. "The Office of the Future - Part 2." Computer Decisions, vol. 11, no. 8, August 1979, pp. 68-69, 71-72, 74-75.

Dunning, Bonnie Walton. "The Evolution of the Professional Computer Systems Analyst Ethic." Eurocomp Conference Proceedings, 1974, pp. 981-990.

Duro, Aldo. "Humanities Computing Activities in Italy." Computers and the Humanities, vol. 3, no. 1, September 1969, pp. 49-52.

Dyba, Jerome E. "Law Enforcement Management in Anne Arundel County, Maryland." Law and Computer Technology, May 1969, pp. 16-25.

Dynes, Russell R., and others. Social Problems: Dissension and Deviation in an Industrial Society. New York, New York: Oxford University Press, 1964.

Eames, C., and Eames, R. A Computer Perspective. Cambridge, Massachusetts: Harvard University Press, 1973, 174 pp.

Earl, Michael J. "What Microprocessors Mean." Management Today, December 1978, pp. 66-73, 120.

Eberstadt, E. "Myths of the Food Crisis." The New York Review of Books, 19 February 1976, pp. 32-37.

Eckstein, Otto, and McLagan, Donald L. "National Economic Models Help Business to Focus on the Future." Computer Decisions, vol. 3, no. 10, October 1971, pp. 12-17.

Edds, J.A. "EDP Without Tears." Business Quarterly, Spring 1971, pp. 26-34.

Eddy, Amos. "The City...Because There Are People." In Proceedings of the 1974 International Conference on Systems, Man and Cybernetics, pp. 361-364. New York, New York: The Institute of Electrical and Electronics Engineers, Inc., October 1974.

Egbert, Robert L. "The Computer in Education: Malefactor or Benefactor." AFIPS Conference Proceedings, FJCC, vol. 24, 1963, pp. 619-630.

Ehrle, Raymond A. "Decision-Making in an Automated Age." Personnel Journal, November 1963, pp. 492-494.

Eigen, Lewis D. "High-School Reactions to Programed Instruction." Phi Delta Kappan, vol. 44, March 1963, pp. 282-285.

Ein-Dor, Phillip, and Segev, Eli. "Strategic Planning for Management Information Systems." Management Science, vol. 24, no. 15, November 1978, pp. 1631-1641.

"Electronic Banking - A Retreat from the Cashless Society." Business Week, 18 April 1977, pp. 80-83, 86-87, 90.

Elgin, Buane S., and Bushnell, Robert A. "The Limits of Complexity: Are Bureauracies Becoming Unmanageable?" The Futurist, December 1977, pp. 337-349.

Eliason, Alan L., and Kitts, Kent D. Business Computer Systems and Applications. Palo Alto, California: Science Research Associates, 1974, 335 pp.

Elizur, D. Adapting to Innovation. Jerusalem, Israel: Jerusalem Academic Press, 1970.

Elliott, Bob, and Goulding, Ray. "The Day the Computers Got Waldon Ashenfelter." Atlantic, November 1967, pp. 58-61. Science fiction.

Ellis, Allan B. The Use and Misuse of Computers in Education. New York, New York: McGraw-Hill Book Company, 1974, 226 pp.

Ellison, Alfred. "Problems of Applying Computer Technology to Teacher Education." Educational Technology, vol. 10, no. 11, November 1970, pp. 35-39.

Ellison, J.R., and Taylor, F.E. Where Next For Computer Security? New York, New York: International Publishing Service, 1974.

Ellul, Jacques. The Technological Society. New York, New York: Alfred A. Knopf, Inc., 1964.

Emery, J.C. "An Overview of Management Information Systems." Data Base, vol. 5, nos. 2-4, Winter 1973, pp. 1-15.

Engberg, Edward. "A Public View of Privacy." *The Center Magazine*, January 1968, pp. 69-73.

Engelhardt, H. Tristram, Jr. "The Roots of Science and Ethics." *Hastings Center Report*, June 1976, pp. 35-38.

Entmacher, P.S., and Gutman, J.S. "Computerized Insurance Records." *Hastings Center Report*, November 1973, pp. 8-10.

Epstein, Sam, and Epstein, Beryl. *The First Book of Teaching Machines*. New York, New York: Franklin Watts, Inc., 1961, 50 pp.

Erikson, Raymond F. "Musical Analysis and the Computer: A Report on Some Current Approaches and the Outlook for the Future." *Computers and the Humanities*, vol. 3, no. 2, November 1968, pp. 87-104.

Ernst, M.L., and Schwartz, A.H. *Privacy: The Right to Be Left Alone*. New York, New York: The Macmillan Company, 1962.

Erwin, Sam J., Jr. "The Computer and Individual Privacy." *Vital Speeches of the Day*, vol. 33, 1 May 1967, pp. 421-426.

_____. "Announcement of Hearings on Computers, Data Banks, and the Bill of Rights." *Congressional Report*, 8 February 1971, pp. 2024-2026.

Evans, Ned. "Quiet Revolution at the Supermarket." *Think*, vol. 45, no. 4, July-August 1979, pp. 4-9.

Ewald, W.R., Jr., ed. *Environment and Change: The Next Fifty Years*. Bloomington, Indiana: Indiana University Press, 1968.

Ewing, J.S., and Murphy, J. "Impact of Automation on United States Retail Food Distribution." *Journal of Retailing*, vol. 41, Spring 1965, pp. 38-47.

Exley, Charles E., Jr. "People Costs in Computers and Data Processing: Predicament, Predilection, and Prediction." *Computers and People*, vol. 27, no. 4, April 1978, pp. 7-8, 17, 22.

Exton, William, Jr. "Computer Output Error and Loss of Credibility." Part 1. *The National Underwriter*, 1 January 1977, pp. 9-11.

_____. "Computer Output Error and Loss of Credibility." Part 2. *The National Underwriter*, 8 January 1977, pp. 13-15.

_____. "Can We Afford to Economize on Accuracy?" *Administration Management*, July 1977, pp. 22-23, 62, 64-65.

Fabun, D. *The Dynamics of Change*. Englewood Cliffs, New Jersey: Prentice-Hall, Inc., 1967.

Fachs, V.R. "Fallacies and Facts about Automation." New York Times Magazine, 7 April 1963, p. 27.

"Facts About Mr. Buckley's Amendment." American Education, vol. 13, no. 5, June 1977, pp. 6-9.

Fadiman, Clifton. "Please Tap My Wire, I Like It!" Holiday, July 1964, pp. 12, 14, 16-17.

Fano, Robert M. "On the Social Role of Computer Communications." Proceedings of the IEEE, vol. 60, no. 11, November 1972, pp. 1249-1253.

Fanwick, Charles. "Maintaining Privacy of Computerized Data." Santa Monica, California: System Development Corporation, Report SP-2647, 1 December 1966.

———. "Computer Safeguards: How Safe Are They?" SDC Magazine, vol. 10, nos. 7-8, July-August 1967, pp. 26-28.

Farmer, James. "Computerized Voting: Many Happy Returns?" Computer Decisions, vol. 6, no. 11, November 1974, pp. 20-23.

Farmer, James; Springer, Colby; and Strumwasser, Michael. "Cheating the Vote-Count Systems." Datamation, vol. 16, no. 5, May 1970, pp. 76-77, 79-80.

Farney, Dennis. "Machine Politics, 1975." Smithsonian, October 1974, pp. 62-68.

Farr, M.A.L. Security for Computer Systems. Manchester, England: NCC Publications, 1972.

Farr, Robert. The Electronic Criminals. New York, New York: McGraw-Hill Book Company, 1975, 194 pp.

Faunce, William A. "Automation in the Automobile Industry: Some Consequences for In-Plant Social Structure." American Sociological Review, vol. 23, August 1958, pp. 401-407.

———. "Automation and the Division of Labor." Social Problems, vol. 13, Fall 1965, pp. 149-160.

———. Problems of an Industrial Society. New York, New York: McGraw-Hill Book Company, 1968.

Featheringham, Tom R. "Computerized Conferencing and Human Communication." IEEE Transactions on Professional Communication, vol. 20, no. 4, December 1977, pp. 207-213.

Feigenbaum, Donald S. "Systems Engineering and Management: Operating Framework of the Future." Journal of Systems Management, vol. 22, no. 8, August 1971, pp. 8-15.

Feigenbaum, E.A., and Feldman, Julian, eds. Computers and Thought. New York, New York: McGraw-Hill Book Company, 1963, 535 pp.

Feinman, Harvey B. "Computers in Complex Litigation." Computer Decisions, vol. 10, no. 4, April 1978, pp. 46, 48.

Feistel, Horst. "Cyptography and Computer Privacy." Scientific American, vol. 228, no. 5, May 1973, pp. 15-23.

Feldhusen, John F. "Taps for Teaching Machines." Phi Delta Kappan, vol. 44, March 1963, pp. 265-267.

Feldhusen, John F., and Birt, Andrew T. "A Study of Nine Methods of Presentation of Programmed Learning Material." Journal of Educational Research, vol. 55, no. 9, June-July 1962, pp. 461-466.

Feldhusen, John F.; Ramharter, Hazel; and Birt, Andrew T. "The Teacher vs. Programed Learning." Wisconsin Journal of Education, vol. 95, no. 3, November 1962, pp. 8-10.

Feldman, David H., and Sears, Pauline S. "Effects of Computer-Assisted Instruction on Children's Behavior." Educational Technology, vol. 10, no. 3, March 1970, pp. 11-14.

Felkenes, George T. "Can the Computer Save our Courts?" Datamation, vol. 17, no. 6, June 1971, pp. 36-39.

Fellegi, I.P. "On the Question of Statistical Confidentiality." Journal of the American Statistical Association, vol. 67, no. 337, March 1972, pp. 7-18.

Felsenstein, Lee. "The Tom Swift Terminal, A 'Convivial' Cybernetic Device." In Computer Technology to Reach the People: Digest of Papers, pp. 203-205. New York, New York: The Institute of Electrical and Electronics Engineers, Inc., Spring COMPCON75, IEEE Catalog No. 75CH0920-9C, February 1975.

Fenchel, R.R., and Weizenbaum, J. Computers and Computation. San Francisco, California: W.H. Freeman and Company, 1971.

Ferguson, Richard L. "Computer Assistance for Individualizing Instuction." Computers and Automation, vol. 19, no. 3, March 1970, pp. 27-29.

Ferkiss, Victor C. Technological Man: The Myth and the Reality. New York, New York: George Braziller, Inc., 1969.

_____. The Future of Technological Civilization. New York, New York: George Braziller, 1974.

Ferranti, B. Living with the Computer. London, England: Oxford University Press, 1971.

Ferrence, T.P. "Can Personnel Selection be Computerized?" Personnel, vol. 45, November 1968, pp. 50-55.

Ferry, W.H. "Must We Rewrite the Constitution to Control Technology?" Saturday Review, vol. 51, 2 March 1968, pp. 50-54.

Fiege, H. Reynold, Jr., and others. "An Experimental Anatomy Computer System." <u>Computers and Biomedical Research</u>, vol. 2, no. 4, June 1969, pp. 373-384.

Filep, Robert T. "Teaching Machines and Programmed Instruction." <u>Audiovisual Communication Review</u>, vol. 11, 1963, pp. 145-148.

Finerman, Aaron, ed. <u>University Education in Computing Science</u>. New York, New York: Academic Press, 1968.

_____. "Professionalism in the Computer Field." <u>Communications of the ACM</u>, January 1975, pp. 4-8.

Fink, D.G. <u>Computers and the Human Mind: An Introduction to Artificial Intelligence</u>. Garden City, New York: Doubleday and Company, 1966.

Finke, Walter W. "Information: Dilemma or Deliverance?" <u>Computers and Automation</u>, vol. 15, no. 8, August 1966, pp. 22-25.

Finn, James D. "Automation and Education: I. General Aspects." <u>Audio-Visual Communication Review</u>, vol. 5, Winter 1957, pp. 343-360.

_____. "Automation and Education: II. Automatizing the Classroom." <u>Audio-Visual Communication Review</u>, vol. 5, Spring 1957, pp. 451-467.

Firschein, Oscar, and others. "Intelligent Machines Are on the Way." <u>IEEE Spectrum</u>, July 1974, pp. 41-48.

Fitzgibbon, Norinne, and Grate, John H. "CAI: Where Do We Go From Here?" <u>Elementary English</u>, vol. 47, no. 7, pp. 917-921.

Fitzhugh, Gilbert W. "Automatic Data Processing in the Department of Defense." <u>Computers and Automation</u>, vol. 19, no. 12, December 1970, pp. 21-24.

Flato, Linda. "EFT and Crime." <u>Computer Decisions</u>, vol. 6, no. 10, October 1974, pp. 30-33.

_____. "A Crisis of Identity." <u>Computer Decisions</u>, vol. 8, no. 5, May 1976, pp. 22-24, 26.

_____. "Postal Automation: Millions for Zip." <u>Computer Decisions</u>, vol. 8, no. 9, September 1976, pp. 22-26, 28-29.

Flato, Linda, and Wiener, Hesh. "Washington Slept Here." <u>Computer Decisions</u>, vol. 6, no. 11, November 1974, pp. 28, 30, 32, 37.

Fletcher, Joseph. <u>Situation Ethics, The New Morality</u>. Philadelphia, Pennsylvania: Westminister Press, 1966.

Flick, F. "Does Automation Cause Unemployment?" <u>Vital Speeches of the Day</u>, 15 Febrary 1962, pp. 280-281.

Florman, S.C. "In Praise of Technology." Harper's, November 1975, pp. 53-72.

Fondiller, Robert. "In the Year 2001: Surgery by Computer." Computers and Automation, vol. 19, no. 6, June 1970, pp. 36-40.

Forrester, Jay W. Urban Dynamics. Cambridge, Massachusetts: MIT Press, 1969.

_____. World Dynamics. Cambridge, Massachusetts: Wright-Allen Press, 1971, 142 pp.

_____. "Limits to Growth Revisited." Journal of the Franklin Institute, vol. 300, no. 2, August 1975, pp. 107-111.

Forsythe, Alan L., and Stansbury, Philip, Mrs. "A Third Grader Meets a Computer." Independent School Bulletin, vol. 30. no. 4, May 1971, pp. 51-53.

"Forty-Nine Computer People on the Social Responsibility of Computer Scientists." Computers and Automation, September 1958, pp. 6, 26, 28.

Foster, Caxton C. "Data Banks - A Position Paper." Computers and Automation, vol. 20, no. 3, March 1971, pp. 28-30.

_____. "The Next Three Generations." Computer, March-April 1972, pp. 39-42.

Foster, David F. "Computers and Social Change: Uses and Misuses." Computers and Automation, vol. 19, no. 8, August 1970, pp. 31-33.

Foster, K.E. "Job Worth and the Computer." Personnel Journal, vol. 47, September 1968, pp. 619-626.

Fox, R.G. "The Application of Computers and Technology to Training." Gaithersburg, Maryland: IBM Corporation, Report FSC-70-6019, October 1970.

Foy, Nancy. The Sun Never Sets on IBM: The Culture and Folklore of IBM World Trade. New York, New York: William Morrow, 1975.

"France is Ready to Clamp Down on Computer Abuses of Privacy." Datamation, vol. 23, no. 4, April 1977, pp. 162-164.

Frances, Leslie. "Money Happy Returns." Computer Decisions, vol. 8, no. 11, November 1976, pp. 24, 26. Checkless, cashless society.

Frank, Ronald A. "Not Only DPers Gulity of DP Crime, Expert Warns." Computerworld, vol. 12, no. 47, 20 November 1978, pp. 1-2.

Franke, H.W. Computer Graphics, Computer Art. London, England: Phaidon Press, 1971.

Frankel, Charles. The Love of Anxiety. New York, New York: Harper and Row, Publishers, 1961.

_____. "The Nature and Sources of Irrationalism." Science, 1 June 1973, pp. 927-931.

Frankena, W.K. Ethics. 2nd edition. Englewood Cliffs, New Jersey: Prentice-Hall, Inc., 1973

Free, John. "Microprocessors: Tiny Overseers That Run Everything - From Cars to Ovens." Popular Science, March 1977, pp. 90-93.

Freed, Roy N. "Legal Aspects of Computer Use in Medicine." Law and Contemporary Problems, vol. 32, no. 4, Autumn 1967, pp. 674-706.

_____. "Computer Fraud: A Management Trap." Business Horizons, June 1969, pp. 25-30.

_____. "Get the Computer System You Want." Harvard Business Review, vol. 47, no. 6, November-December 1969, pp. 99-108.

_____. "A Legal Structure for a National Medical Data Center." Boston University Law Review, vol. 49, Winter 1969, pp. 79-94.

Freiberger, Stephen, and Chew, Paul. Consumer's Guide to Personal Computing and Microcomputers. Rochelle Park, New Jersey: Hayden Book Company, 1978.

Freiberger, W.F., and Prayer, W., eds. Application of Digitial Computers. Boston, Massachusetts: Ginn and Company, 1963.

French, Nancy. "The Privacy Commission: One Year Later." Computerworld, vol. 10, no. 28, 12 July 1976, pp. 1, 8.

_____. "Parker Hits Security Specialists for Lack of Progress." Computerworld, vol. 11, no. 25, 20 June 1977, p. 21.

Fried, Charles. An Anatomy of Values: Problems of Personal and Social Choice. Cambridge, Massachusetts: Harvard University Press, 1970.

Fried, Louis. "When Is the Right Time to Computerize?" The Office, September 1973, pp. 108-110, 112-113.

Friedberg, Richard M. "A Learning Machine: Part I." IBM Journal of Research and Development, vol. 2, no. 1, January 1958, pp. 2-13.

Friedberg, Richard M.; Dunham, Bradford; and North, James H. "A Learning Machine: Part II." IBM Journal of Research and Development, vol. 3, no. 3, July 1959, pp. 282-287.

Friedenberg, Edgar Z. "Thoughts on Liberty and Rancor." Harper's, June 1975, pp. 41-46.

_____. The Disposal of Liberty and Other Industrial Wastes. Garden City, New York: Doubleday and Company, Inc., 1976.

Friedlander, Gordon C. "Computer-Controlled Vehicular Traffic." IEEE Spectrum, vol. 6, no. 2, February 1969, pp. 30-43.

Friedlander, M.W. The Conduct of Science. Englewood Cliffs, New Jersey: Prentice-Hall, Inc., 1972.

Friedman, R.C. "EDP and the Law." Data Management, August 1972, pp. 14-15.

Frielink, A.B., ed. Economics of Informatics. New York, New York: Elsevier-North Holland, 1975.

Fritz, Barkley, and Lansberry, Charles R. "Ship Modeling with Interactive Graphics." Datamation, vol. 21, no. 12, December 1975, pp. 54-58.

Fromer, Robert. "Distinction between CAI and CMI Systems." Educational Technology, vol. 12, no. 5, May 1972, pp. 30-31.

Fromm, Erich. The Sane Society. New York, New York: Holt, Rinehart and Winston, 1955.

_____. The Revolution of Hope: Toward a Humanized Technology. New York, New York: Harper and Row, Publishers, 1968.

Fulbright, J. William. "The Decline - and Possible Fall - of Contitutional Democracy in America." Computers and Automation, vol. 20, no. 6, June 1971, pp. 20-24.

Gabor, Dennis. The Mature Society. New York, New York: Praeger Publishers, Inc., 1972.

Gabrieli, E.R. "The Right of Privacy and Medical Computing." Datamation, vol. 16, no. 4, April 1970, pp. 173, 176, 178.

Galanter, Eugene, ed. Automatic Teaching: The State of the Art. New York, New York: John Wiley and Sons, 1958, 198 pp.

Galbraith, John Kenneth. The Affluent Society. Boston, Massachusetts: Houghton Mifflin Company, 1958.

_____. The New Industrial State. Boston, Massachusetts: Houghton Mufflin Company, 1967.

Gallagher, Cornelius E. "Efficiency - Purchased at the Price of Privacy." Banking, April 1968, pp. 38-39.

_____. "Recapturing Democracy and Privacy from the Computer." Data Management, vol. 8, no. 1, January 1970, pp. 34-38.

_____. "Personal Privacy, Data Security, and a Free America." Congressional Record, 23 September 1970, pp. 33530-33532. Speech by Frank Horton.

Gallagher, Michael; Johnston, Marvin A.; and Cook, James R. "Industry Disenchated with DP Education 'Fairy Tale.'" Data Management, vol. 16, no. 12, December 1978, pp. 62-66.

Gardner, Richard. "The Shadow, Buck Rogers, and the Home Computer." Byte, vol. 1, no. 2, October 1975, pp. 58-60.

Gardner, W. David. "Big Boom in Minicomputers." Dun's Review, vol. 112, no. 1, July 1978, pp. 70-72, 75.

Garg, Devendra P. "Technology Assessment and Social Choice: A Course." Computers and Society, Spring 1974, pp. 2-3.

Garrett, Lewis E. "Primer on Artificial Intelligence." Creative Computing, March-April 1976, pp. 20-24.

Garrison, William A., and Ramamoorthy, C.V. "Privacy and Security in Data Banks." Austin, Texas: University of Texas, Electronics Research Center, Technical Memorandum 24, 2 November 1970.

Garrity, John T. "Top Management and Computer Profits." Harvard Business Review, vol. 41, no. 4, July-August 1963, pp. 6-12, 172-174.

Gavin, James M. "The Social Impact of Information Systems." Computers and Automation, vol. 18, no. 7, July 1969, pp. 16-18.

Gaylin, Willard. "From Twain to Freud: An Examination of Conscience." Hastings Center Report, August 1976, pp. 5-8.

Gellman, Harvey S. "Using the Computer to Steal." Computers and Automation, vol. 20, no. 4, April 1971, pp. 16-19.

George, Frank H. "The Urgent Need to Rethink the Use of the Computer in Industry." Computers and Automation, vol. 20, no. 12, December 1971, pp. 19-21.

_____. Computers, Science and Society. Buffalo, New York: Prometheus Books, 1972.

_____. Machine Takeover: The Growing Threat to Human Freedom in a Computer-Controlled Society. Elmsford, New York: Pergamon Press, Inc., 1977.

George, Frank H., and Humphries, J.D., eds. The Robots are Coming. Manchester, England: NCC Publications, 1974.

George, Mary. "The Press Button Age." Electron Power, vol. 22, no. 5, May 1976, pp. 307-309.

Gerard, Ralph W. "Computers and Education." AFIPS Conference Proceedings, FJCC, vol. 27, Part 2, November-December 1965, pp. 11-16.

_____., ed. Computers and Education. New York, New York: McGraw-Hill Book Company, 1967.

Gerrold, David. When Harlie Was One. Garden City, New York: Nelson Doubleday, 1972. Science fiction.

Gerson, Elihu M. "Directory of Researchers in Computers and Society." Computers and Society, vol. 8, no. 4, Winter 1977, pp. 5-9.

Gerstein, Robert S. "Privacy and Self-Incrimination." Ethics, vol. 80, no. 2, January 1970, pp. 87-101.

Gewirth, Alan. "Ethics." In The New Encyclopaedia Britannica, Macropaedia, Volume 6, pp. 976-998. Chicago, Illinois: Encyclopaedia Britannica, Inc., 1974.

Gibson, C.F., and Nolan, R.L. "Managing the Four Stages of EDP Growth." Harvard Business Review, vol. 52, no. 1, January-February 1974, pp. 76-88.

Gilchrist, Bruce, and Shenkin, Arlaana. "The Impact of Sanners on Employment in Supermarkets." Computers and Society, vol. 10, no. 1, Summer 1979, pp. 4-8.

Gilchrist, Bruce, and Wessel, M.R. Government Regulation of the Computer Industry. Montvale, New Jersey: AFIPS Press, 1972.

Gildersleeve, Thomas R. "Who Owns the Data?" Infosystems, October 1976, pp. 70, 72.

Gillam, Richard. "Intellectuals and Power." The Center Magazine, May-June 1977, pp. 15-30.

Gillespie, Robert, and Shaw, Alan. "Computers and Society - A Course." Computers and Society, Spring 1975, pp. 7-8.

Girsdansky, M.B. "Cryptology, the Computer and Data Privacy." Computers and Automation, vol. 21, no. 4, April 1972, pp. 12-19.

Glaseman, S.; Turn, R.; and Gaines, R.S. "Problem Areas in Computer Security Assessment." Santa Monica, California: The RAND Corporation, Report P-5822, February 1977, 29 pp.

Glaser, E.; Rosenblatt, D.; and Wood, M.K. "The Design of a Federal Statistical Data Center." American Statistician, February 1967, pp. 12-20.

Glauberman, M.H. "Computers in Education - An RCA Viewpoint." Educational Technology, vol. 9, no. 8, September 1969, pp. 63-66.

Glaza, Tom. "Computer-Based Manufacturing Control." Viewpoint, September-October 1978, pp. 14-16.

Gloye, Euguene E., and Marcus, Rudolph J. "Drug Effect Prediction by Computer." Science, vol. 169, no. 3940, 3 July 1970, pp. 89-91.

Goetowski, Charles R. "Computer-Assisted Electrocardiography: Past, Present, and Future." In Digest of Papers, pp. 311-314. New York, New York: The Institute of Electrical and Electronics Engineers, Inc., Fall COMPCON76, IEEE Catalog No. 76CH1115-5C, September 1976.

Goldbeck, Robert A., and Campbell, Vincent N. "The Effects on Response Mode and Response Difficulty on Programmed Learning." *Journal of Educational Psychology*, vol. 53, no. 3, 1962, pp. 110-118.

Goldberg, A.J. "Challenges of the Second Industrial Revolution." *Management Review*, vol. 50, May 1961, pp. 51-53.

Goldberg, Robert P. "How to Implement Systems Which Comply with the Privacy Act of 1974." In *How to Make Computers Easier to Use: Digest of Papers*, pp. 37-40. New York, New York: The Institute of Electrical and Electronics Engineers, Inc., Fall COMPCON75, IEEE Catalog No. 75CH0988-6C, 9-11 September 1975.

Goldstein, Robert C. "The Costs of Privacy." *Datamation*, vol. 21, no. 10, October 1975, pp. 65-69.

Goldstein, Robert C., and Nolan, Richard L. "Personal Privacy Versus the Corporate Computer." *Harvard Business Review*, vol. 53, no. 2, March-April 1975, pp. 62-70.

Goldstine, Herman H. "Social Implications of the Computer." *Annals of the New York Academy of Sciences*, vol. 184, 7 June 1971, pp. 201-205.

_____. *The Computer from Pascal to Von Neumann*. Princeton, New Jersey: Princeton University Press, 1972, 378 pp.

Goldwater, Barry M., Jr. "Data Havens: International Privacy Threat." *Computer Decisions*, vol. 9, no. 6, June 1977, pp. 22-24.

Goldworthy, A.W. "INSURE: An Online Insurance System." *Australian Computer Journal*, vol. 4, no. 3, August 1972, pp. 127-134.

_____. "Computers and Privacy: A Review of the Younger Committee Report." *Australian Computer Journal*, vol. 5, no. 1, February 1973, pp. 3-7.

_____. "Today and Tomorrow: The Need for Effective Dissemination of Knowledge About Computers." *Sixth Australian Computer Conference Proceedings*, 20-24 May 1974, pp. 140-152.

Goodlad, John I.; O'Toole, John F., Jr.; and Tyler, Louise L. *Computers and Information Systems in Education*. New York, New York: Harcourt, Brace, and World, 1966.

Gopalakrishman, P., and Narayanan, K.S. *Computers in India: An Overview*. Thompson, Connecticut: InterCulture Associates, 1976.

Goshay, Robert C. *Information Technology in the Insurance Industry*. Homewood, Illinois: Richard D. Irwin, Inc., 1964.

Gotlieb, C.C., and Borodin, A. *Social Issues in Computing*. New York, New York: Academic Press, Inc., 1973, 284 pp.

───. "Social Issues in Computing - The Course." *Computers and Society*, Spring 1974, p. 2.

Gottheimer, Debra. "Computer Graphics: 'One Image Is Worth 10,000 Printouts.'" *Administrative Management*, vol. 39, no. 7, July 1978, pp. 57-60, 63, 103.

Gould, Jay W. *The Technical Elite*. New York, New York: August M. Kelley, 1966.

Government Dossier (Survey of Information Contained in Government Files). United States Senate, Subcommittee on Administrative Practice and Procedure, Committee on the Judiciary, 90th Congress, 1st Session, November 1967.

Gradel, Thomas J. "Coming: A Cashless Society?" *Electronic Age*, Winter 1968-69, pp. 31-34.

Graham, J. Wesley. "Computers, a Revolution in Secondary Education." *Computers and Automation*, vol. 16, no. 3, March 1967, pp. 23-24, 56.

Graham, Neill. *The Mind Tool: Computers and Their Impact on Society*. New York, New York: West Publishing Company, 1976, 263 pp.

Graham, Otis L., Jr., an interview with. "Planning the Society." *The Center Magazine*, May-June 1977, pp. 8-14.

Graham, Robert M. "Protection in an Information Processing Utility." *Communications of the ACM*, vol. 11, no. 5, May 1968, pp. 365-369.

Graves, Clare W. "A Systems View of Values Problems." In *Record of the IEEE Systems Science and Cybernetics Conference*, pp. 27-33. New York, New York: The Institute of Electrical and Electronics Engineers, Inc., October 1969.

Gravin, James M. "The Social Impact of Information Systems." *Computers and Automation*, vol. 18, no. 7, July 1969, pp. 16-18.

Grayson, Lawrence P. "Computer-Assisted Instruction and its Implications for University Education." Yorktown Heights, New York: IBM Corporation, Report RC-2169, August 1969, 15 pp.

───. "Education Beyond the Horizon." *Science*, vol. 170, 23 December 1970, pp. 1376-1382.

Green, Harold P. "Human Values in a Technological Society." *Dimensions*, Winter 1971, pp. 19-23.

Greenawalt, Kent. "The Burger Court and Claims of Privacy." *Hastings Center Report*, August 1976, pp. 19-20.

Greenberg, Donald P. "Computer Graphics in Architecture." *Scientific American*, vol. 230, no. 5, May 1974, pp. 98-106.

Greenberg, H.Y. "Privacy Versus the Computer." Banker's Monthly, vol. 86, August 1969, pp. 37-38, 52.

Greenberger, Martin, ed. Computers and the World of the Future. Cambridge, Massachusetts: MIT Press, 1962, 340 pp.

_____., ed. Computers, Communications, and the Public Interest. Baltimore, Maryland: John Hopkins University Press, 1971, 312 pp.

_____., and others. "Modeling and the Political Process." Computers and Society, Spring 1976, pp. 3-14.

Greenblott, Bernard J., and Hsiao, Mu Y. "Where is Technology Taking Us in Data Processing Systems." Poughkeepsie, New York: IBM Corporation, Technical Report 00.2460, 13 July 1973.

Grindlay, Andrew. "You and the Computer - Problems of Data Processing: Are They Serious?" Business Quarterly, vol. 41, Autumn 1976, pp. 93-95.

Groppuso, Fred, and Utrich, Robert C. "Industrial Security: Its Intelligent Organization." Computers and People, vol. 26, no. 3, March 1977, pp. 12-13.

Grosch, Herbert R.J. "Who Owns the Data?" Computerworld, 26 April 1976, p. 17.

_____. "Our Freedom Is Our Strength." Computer Decisions, vol. 10, no. 1, January 1978, pp. 58, 61-62.

Gross, Martin. The Brain Watchers. New York, New York: Random House, 1962.

Grossman, Jerome H. "Management Information Systems in Medicine." Sloan Management Review, vol. 13, no. 2, Winter 1972, pp. 1-7.

Grosswirth, Marvin. "Leachim the Teaching Robot." Datamation, vol. 20, no. 8, August 1974, pp. 64-67.

Gruenberger, Fred J. "What is the 'Social Responsibilty' Problem?" Santa Monica, California: The RAND Corporation, Report P-3163, July 1965, 8 pp.

_____. Expanding Use of Computers in the 70's. Englewood Cliffs, New Jersey: Prentice-Hall, Inc., 1971.

_____. Computers and the Social Environment. Los Angeles, California: Melville Publishing Company, 1975.

_____. "Who Will Look After the Computing Part of Personal Computing?" Personal Computing, vol. 1, no. 5, September-October 1977, pp. 107-109. Future computing.

Gruenberger, Fred J., and Jaffray, G. Problems for Computer Solution. New York, New York: John Wiley and Sons, Inc., 1965.

Guerrieri, John A., Jr. "Certification - Evolution, Not Revolution." <u>Datamation</u>, vol. 19, no. 11, November 1973, pp. 101-104.

Guertin, Wilson M. "Straight Talk about Computer Information Systems." <u>Educational Technology</u>, vol. 9, no. 7, August 1969, pp. 25-30.

Guilbaud, G.T. <u>What is Cybernetics</u>? New York, New York: Criterion Press, 1959.

Gulley, David A., and Kane, William G. "The Planner's Computer." <u>Datamation</u>, vol. 20, no. 5, May 1974, pp. 64-67.

Gupta, G.K. "Social Implications of Computer Technology." <u>Computers and Society</u>, Winter 1975, pp. 10-12.

Gupta, Roger. "Information Manager: His Role in Corporate Management." <u>Data Management</u>, vol. 12, no. 7, July 1974, pp. 26-29.

Haak, Harold H. "The Evolution of a Metropolitan Data System." <u>Urban Affairs Quarterly</u>, December 1967, pp. 3-13.

Haden, Douglas. <u>Total Business Systems: Computers in Business</u>. St. Paul, Minnesota: West Publishing Company, 1978.

Haga, Enoch, ed. <u>Computer Techniques in Biomedicine and Medicine</u>. Philadelphia, Pennsylvania: Auerbach Publishers, 1973.

Halacy, Daniel S., Jr. <u>Cyborg: Evolution of the Superman</u>. New York, New York: Harper and Row, Publishers, 1965, 207 pp.

_____. <u>Computers: The Machines We Think With</u>. New York, New York: Harper and Row, Publishers, 1969.

Halas, J., ed. <u>Computer Animation</u>. New York, New York: Hastings House Publishers, 1974.

Hall, Keith. "Computer-Assisted Instruction: Problems and Performance." <u>Phi Delta Kappan</u>, vol. 52, no. 10, June 1971, pp. 628-631.

Hall, P.D. "The Computer and Society." <u>Computer Bulletin</u>, vol. 11, no. 3, December 1967, pp. 216-219.

Hallam, Stephen F., and others. "Basic Steps in Developing Simulation Models." <u>Data Management</u>, April 1975, pp. 26-29.

Halloran, Norbert A. "Judicial Data Centers." <u>Law and Computer Technology</u>, April 1969, pp. 9-15.

Hamilton, Peter. <u>Espionage and Subversion in an Industrial Society</u>. London, England: Hatchinson Publishing Group, Ltd., 1967.

Hamilton, William J., and Moses, Michael A. "A Computer-Based Corporate Planning System." *Management Science*, vol. 21, no. 2, October 1974, pp. 148-159.

Hammel, D.G. "An Introduction to Computer-Assisted Instruction." *Modern Data*, vol. 5, no. 10, October 1972, pp. 42-44.

Hammer, Donald. "Automated Operations in a University Library." *College and Research Libraries*, vol. 26, January 1965, pp. 19-29.

Hamming, Richard W. "Intellectual Implications of the Computer Revolution." *American Mathematical Monthly*, January 1963, pp. 9-11.

_____. *Computers and Society*. New York, New York: McGraw-Hill Book Company, 1972, 284 pp.

_____. "The History of Computers to the Year 2000." In *Proceedings of the Joint IBM University of Newcastle upon Tyne Seminar*, pp. 45-57. Newcastle, England: University of Newcastle upon Tyne, 9-12 September 1975.

_____. "Computers in the Coming Society." In *Proceedings of the Joint IBM University of Newcastle upon Tyne Seminar*, pp. 59-76. Newcastle, England: University of Newcastle upon Tyne, 9-12 September 1975.

Hammond, A.L. "Computer-Assisted Instruction: Two Major Demonstrations." *Science*, vol. 176, 1972, pp. 1110-1112.

Hammond, John S., III. "Do's and Don'ts of Computer Models for Planning." *Harvard Business Review*, vol. 52, no. 2, March-April 1974, pp. 110-123.

Hammond, Paul Y. "The Societal Effects of Computers: Partner or Placebo in Policy Analysis." Santa Monica, California: The RAND Corporation, Report P-5539, December 1975, 13 pp.

Handlin, Oscar. "Man and Magic: First Encounters with the Machine." *American Scholar*, vol. 33, no. 3, Summer 1964, pp. 408-419.

_____. "Science and Technology in Popular Culture." *Daedalus*, vol. 94, no. 1, Winter 1965, pp. 156-170.

Hanks, Jerry G. "Knowledge, Bureaucracy and the Computer." *Infosystems*, vol. 24, no. 2, February 1977, pp. 100, 102.

Hanold, Terrance. "An Executive View of MIS." *Datamation*, vol. 18, no. 11, November 1972, pp. 65-71.

Hansen, Duncan N. "CAI Myths that Need to Be Destroyed and CAI Myths that We Ought to Create." Tallahassee, Florida: Florida State University, Computer-Assisted Instruction Center, Technical Memorandum 38, June 1971, 19 pp.

Hansen, Duncan N.; Dick, Walter; and Lippert, Henry. "Computer in Education at Florida State University." *Educational Technology*, vol. 9, no. 4, April 1969, pp. 47-48.

Hansen, Duncan N., and Harvey, William L. "Impact of CAI on Classroom Teachers." Tallahassee, Florida: Florida State University, Computer-Assisted Instruction Center, Technical Memorandum 10, October 1969, 7 pp. Also in *Educational Technology*, vol. 10, no. 2, February 1970, pp. 46-48.

Hansen, James V. "Progress in Health Care Systems." *Journal of Systems Management*, vol. 26, no. 4, April 1975, pp. 14-21.

Hansen, John R. "Evaluating an Awesome Computer Facility." *Infosystems*, vol. 25, no. 1, January 1978, pp. 66-71.

Hapgood, Fred. "Computers Aren't So Smart After All." *Atlantic*, vol. 234, no. 2, August 1974, pp. 37-45.

Hardin, Garrett. "An Evolutionist Looks at Computers." *Datamation*, vol. 15, no. 5, May 1969, pp. 98-109.

_____. *Exploring New Ethics for Survival*. New York, New York: Viking Press, Inc., 1972.

Harman, A.J. *The International Computer Industry: Innovation and Computer Advantage*. Cambridge, Massachusetts: Harvard University Press, 1971.

Harmon, Leon D. "Automatic Recognition of Print and Script." *Proceedings of the IEEE*, vol. 60, no. 10, October 1972, pp. 1165-1176.

Harmon, M. *Sretching Man's Mind: A History of Data Processing*. New York, New York: Mason/Charter Publishers, 1975.

Harrar, George. "The Schizophrenic Computer." *New Englander*, September 1976, pp. 22-23, 40, 42.

Harrington, William G. "Computers and Legal Research." *Law and Computer Technology*, vol. 4, no. 3, May-June 1971, pp. 69-75.

Harrison, Annette. "The Problem of Privacy in the Computer Age: An Overview." Santa Monica, California: The RAND Corporation, Report RM-5495-PR/RC, December 1967, pp. 1-16.

Hartley, J.R., and Woods, Pat. "Some Learning Models for Arithmetic Tasks and Their Use in Computer-Based Learning." *British Journal of Educational Psychology*, vol. 41, no. 2, February 1971, pp. 38-48.

Hartman, Edward. "The Cost of Computer-Assisted Instruction." *Educational Technology*, vol. 11, no. 12, December 1971, pp. 6-7.

Hastings, Susan. "Psychiatric Assessment Via Computer." *Creative Computing*, July-August 1977, p. 34.

Hausrath, A.H. *Venture Simulation in War, Business, and Politics.*
New York, New York: McGraw-Hill Book Company, 1971.

Hawkes, N. *Computer Revolution.* New York, New York: E.P. Dutton,
1973, 216 pp.

Hawkins, C.E., and Devey, D.P. "IBM, the Managing of Employee
Personal Information, and Employee Privacy." Armonk, New York:
IBM Corporation, 18 March 1976, 26 pp.

Head, Robert V. "Management Information Systems: A Critical
Appraisal." *Datamation,* vol. 13, no. 5, May 1967, pp. 22-26.

_____. "The Elusive MIS." *Datamation,* vol. 16, no. 10, September
1970, pp. 22-27.

Hearle, Edward F.R. "The Potential of Electronic Data Processing in
Municipal Government." Santa Monica, California: The RAND
Corporation, Report P-1924-RC, 26 February 1960, 8 pp.

_____. "Can EDP be Applied to all Police Agencies?" Santa Monica,
California: The RAND Corporation, Report P-2454, 1 October 1961,
12 pp.

Hearle, Edward F.R., and Mason, Raymond J. "The Future of Data
Processing in State Government." Santa Monica, California: The
RAND Corporation, Report P-2062-RC, 8 August 1960, 9 pp.

_____. "Data Processing for Cities." Santa Monica, California: The
RAND Corporation, Report P-2492, February 1962, 50 pp.

_____. "A Data-Processing System for State and Local Governments."
Santa Monica, California: The RAND Corporation, Report P-2557,
March 1962, 15 pp.

_____. *A Data-Processing System for State and Local Governments.*
Englewood Cliffs, New Jersey: Prentice-Hall, Inc., 1963.

Hearst, Eliot. "Psychology Across the Chessboard." *Psychology
Today,* vol. 1, no. 2, June 1967, pp. 29-37.

Heilbroner, Robert L. "The American Plan: National Economic
Planning Will Arrive When Businessmen Demand It and Demand It
They Will, To Save the Capitalist System." *New York Times
Magazine,* 25 January 1976, pp. 9, 35-36, 38, 40.

Heinlein, Robert A. *The Moon is a Harsh Mistress.* New York, New
York: G.P. Putnam's Sons, 1966. Science fiction.

Helfgott, Roy B. "EDP and the Office Work Force." *Industrial and
Labor Relations Review,* vol. 19, July 1966, pp. 503-516.

Heller, Christopher E. "EFT and the Prospects for Individual
Privacy." *Datamation,* vol. 21, no. 9, September 1975, pp. 174,
176, 178.

Hemphill, Stuart R. "Protection of Privacy of Computerized Records in the National Crime Information Center." University of Michigan Journal of Law Review, vol. 7, no. 3, Spring 1974, pp. 594-614.

Henderson, Hazel. "Computers: Hardware of Democracy." Forum 70, vol. 2, no. 2, February 1970, pp. 22-25, 46-51.

Henderson, Robert P. "Personal Privacy, Human Dignity and the Computer." In Proceedings of the 1971 Institute in Technical and Industrial Communication, edited by Delbert McGuire, pp. 13-16. Fort Collins, Colorado: Colorado State College, 1971.

_____. "Social Implications of Computerized Information Systems." Computers and Automation, vol. 22, no. 3, March 1973, pp. 11-14, 21.

Herner, Saul, and Vellucci, Mathew J., eds. Selected Federal Computer-Based Information Systems. Washington, D.C.: Information Resources Press, 1972.

Hertlein, Grace C. "Computers and Society: A Current Course Outline for General Education." Computers and People, vol. 24, no. 7, July 1975, pp. 24-26.

Hertz, David B. "Computers and the World Communications Crisis." American Scholar, vol. 35, no. 2, Spring 1966, pp. 265-271.

_____. New Power for Management: Computer Systems and Management Science. New York, New York: McGraw-Hill Book Company, 1969.

Hickey, Albert E. "Teaching With Computers." Training in Business and Industry, vol. 9, no. 4, April 1972, pp. 41-46.

Hickey, Albert E., and Newton, John M. Computer-Assisted Instruction: A Survey of the Literature. 2nd edition. Newburyport, Massachusetts: Entelek, Inc., January 1962.

Hicks, Bruce L. "Will the Computer Kill Education?" Educational Forum, vol. 34, no. 4, March 1970, pp. 307-312.

_____. "Computer Outreach." Computers and Society, Fall 1976, pp. 10-14.

Hicks, Bruce L., and Hunka, S. The Teacher and the Computer. Philadelphia, Pennsylvania: Saunders, 1972.

Hill, R.H., and Furst, N. "Teacher Behavior in CAI Classrooms." Educational Technology, vol. 9, no. 9, September 1969, pp. 60-62.

Hill, Walter A. "The Impact of EDP Systems on Office Employees: Some Empirical Solutions." Academy of Management Journal, vol. 9, no. 1, March 1966, pp. 9-19.

Hilton, Alice Mary. "An Ethos for the Age of Cyberculture." In Data Processing Yearbook - 1965, pp. 25-37. Detroit, Michigan: American Data Processing, Inc., 1964.

_____., ed. *The Evolving Society: The Proceedings of the First Annual Conference on the Cybercultural Revolution - Cybernetics and Automation*. New York, New York: The Institute for Cybercultural Research, 1966, 410 pp.

Hiltz, Starr R., and Turoff, Murray. *Network Nation: Human Communication via Computer*. Reading, Massachusetts: Addison-Wesley Publishing Company, 1978.

Hirch, Phil. "The World's Biggest Data Bank." *Datamation*, vol. 16, no. 5, May 1970, pp. 66-73.

_____. "LEAA: Who Guards the Guardians?" *Datamation*, vol. 17, no. 6, June 1971, pp. 28-31.

_____. "Computer Systems and the Issue of Privacy: How Far Away is 1984?" *Datamation*, vol. 18, no. 12, December 1972, pp. 90-93.

_____. "A 'Conspiracy' to Turn the Mails Back to Private Enterprise." *Datamation*, vol. 23, no. 7, July 1977, pp. 154-157.

Hodge, Bartow. "The Computer in Management Information and Control Systems." *Data Management*, vol. 12, no. 12, December 1974, pp. 26-30.

Hodgson, R.M.; Gelade, G.A.; and Beurle, R.L. "Computers and Urban Society." *Communications of the ACM*, vol. 15, no. 7, July 1972, pp. 652-657.

Hoffberg, Alan. "Coming to Grips with Distributed Processing." *Administrative Management*, vol. 39, no. 5, May 1978, pp. 52-54, 56, 58, 59-62, 64, 66, 68.

Hoffer, E. *The True Believer*. New York, New York: Harper and Row, Publishers, 1951.

Hoffer, William. "Conference Via Computer: A New Way to Hold Your Next Board Meeting." *Association Management*, vol. 29, no. 3, March 1977, pp. 53-56.

Hoffman, Lance J. "Computers and Privacy: A Survey." *Computing Surveys*, vol. 1, no. 2, June 1969, pp. 85-103.

_____., ed. *Security and Privacy in Computer Systems*. Los Angeles, California: Melville Publishing Company, 1973, 422 pp.

_____. "Computer Security: A Course." *Computers and Society*, Winter 1974, pp. 6-8.

_____. "Privacy Laws Affecting System Design." *Computers and Society*, vol. 8, no. 3, Fall 1977, pp. 3-6.

Hoffman, Lance J., and Miller, W.F. "Getting a Personal Dossier from a Statistical Data Bank." *Datamation*, vol. 16, no. 5, May 1970, pp. 74-75.

Hofmann, Adele D. "Confidentiality and the Health Care Records of Children and Youth." Psychiatric Opinion, January 1975, pp. 20-28.

Holden, Constance. "Privacy: Congressional Efforts Are Coming to Fruition." Science, 16 May 1975, pp. 713-715.

Hollings, Ernest F. "An Intelligent, Coordinated Federal Information Policy." Computers and People, vol. 27, nos. 8-9, August-September 1978, pp. 28-30.

Hollingworth, Dennis; Glaseman, Steve; and Hopwood, Marsha. "Security Test and Evaluation Tools: An Approach to Operating System Security Analysis." Santa Monica, California: The RAND Corporation, Report P-5298, September 1974, 26 pp.

Hollom, J.Q. "Computers in Banking." Computers and Automation, vol. 21, no. 8, August 1972, pp. 20-21.

Holmes, Edith. "Election Systems Win Vote Count Race." Computerworld, vol. 8, no. 46, 13 November 1974, pp. 1-2.

_____. "Mini Report on Medicine." Computerworld, vol. 9, no. 15, April 1975, pp. 7-11.

_____. "Parker Warns Congress DP Crime on Increase." Computerworld, vol. 12, no. 28, 10 July 1978, p. 7.

Holmes, James D., and Awad, Elias M. Perspectives on Electronic Data Processing. Englewood Cliffs, New Jersey: Prentice-Hall, Inc., 1972.

Holoien, Martin O. Computers and Their Societal Impact. New York, New York: John Wiley and Sons, Inc., 1977, 264 pp.

Holt, H.O., and Stevenson, F.L. "Human Performance Considerations in Complex Systems." Science, 18 March 1977, pp. 1205-1209.

Holton, Gerald. "Scientific Optimism and Societal Concerns." Hastings Center Report, December 1975, pp. 39-47.

Holtzman, Wayne H., ed. Computer-Assisted Instruction, Testing, and Guidance. New York, New York: Harper and Row, Publishers, 1970.

Hondius. Emerging Data Processing in Europe. New York, New York: Elsevier-North Holland Publishing Company, 1975.

Hoos, Ida Russakoff. "When the Computer Takes Over the Office." Harvard Business Review, vol. 38, no. 4, July-August 1960, pp. 102-112.

Hoppe, R., and Berv, E. "Measurement of Attitude Toward Automation." Personal Psychology, vol. 20, no. 1, 1967, pp. 65-70.

Horowitz, E.; Morgan, H.L.; and Shaw, A.C. "Computers and Society: A Proposed Course for Computer Scientists." Communications of the ACM, April 1972, pp. 257-261.

Horton, Forest W., Jr. "The United States Budget and the Computer." Datamation, vol. 16, no. 4, April 1970, pp. 165-168.

_____. "Personal Privacy, Data Security, and a Free America." Congressional Record, 23 September 1970, pp. 33530-33532.

_____. "Building Block Approach: Key to Federal Management Systems." Journal of Systems Management, vol. 22, no. 10, October 1971, pp. 38-41.

Hough, John B. "An Analysis of the Efficiency and Effectiveness of Selected Aspects of Machine Instruction." Journal of Educational Research, vol. 55, no. 9, June-July 1962, pp. 467-471.

Hough, John B., and Revsin, Bernard. "Programed Instruction at the College Level: A Study of Several Factors Influencing Learning." Phi Delta Kappan, vol. 44, March 1963, pp. 286-291.

Houser, Thomas J. "A Selected Booklist on the Social Implications of Computing." Computers and Education, vol. 1, no. 3, 1977, pp. 141-149.

"How Computers are Making Congressmen More Effective." Government Executive, vol. 9, no. 6, June 1977, pp. 46-48.

Howard, John A. "Vital Issues and Valid Ethics: Birth, Life and Death." Vital Speeches of the Day, 1 November 1973, pp. 45-48.

Howe, Eric James. "Computer Security: Public and User Attitudes." Internal Auditor, vol. 35, no. 2, April 1978, pp. 79-85.

Howells, W.W. "The Importance of Being Human." Computers and Automation, vol. 21, no. 10, October 1972, pp. 12-14, 41-42.

Hubbard, George U. "Conversational Computing for Housewives." Datamation, vol. 15, no. 3, March 1969, pp. 34-35.

Hughes, J.L., and McNamara, W.J. "A Comparative Study of Programed and Conventional Instruction in Industry." Journal of Applied Psychology, vol. 45, no. 4, 1961, pp. 225-231.

Hugh-Jones, E.M. The Push-Button World: Automation Today. Norman, Oklahoma: University of Oklahoma Press, 1956.

Hullfish, William R. "Use of Drill Programs to Teach Abstract Concepts by Computer-Assisted Instructions." Audiovisual Instruction, vol. 16, no. 2, February 1971, pp. 35-36.

Humble, John. "A Practical Approach to Social Responsibility." Management Review, vol. 67, no. 5, May 1978, pp. 18-22.

Hunt, Earl B. Artificial Intelligence. New York, New York: Academic Press, 1975.

Huntsinger, Jerald E. "Seven Thoughts on Writing a Computer Letter: Name Game." <u>Fund Raising Management</u>, vol. 9, no. 4, September-October 1978, pp. 52, 54.

Huxley, Aldous. <u>Brave New World Revisited</u>. New York, New York: Harper and Row, Publishers, 1958.

Hyatt, David. "An Executive's Guide to Computers." <u>Industry Week</u>, vol. 197, no. 1, 3 April 1978, pp. 43-51, 54-56.

IBM Corporation. <u>Symposium on Introducing the Computer into the Humanities</u>. Publication G320-1044-0, June-July 1969, 132 pp.

_____. <u>The Considerations of Data Security in a Computer Environment</u>. Publication G520-2169-0, July 1970.

_____. <u>Computer Approach to Marketing Applications for Consumer Packaged Goods Manufacturers</u>. Publication GE20-0351-0, January 1971, 65 pp.

_____. <u>The Considerations of Physical Security in a Computer Environment</u>. Publication G520-2700-0, October 1972, 37 pp.

_____. <u>IBM Data Security Symposium, April 1973</u>. Publication G520-2838-0, April 1973.

_____. <u>Forty-Two Suggestions for Improving Security in Data Processing Operations</u>. Publication G520-2797-0, October 1973, 19 pp.

_____. <u>Data Security and Data Processing, Volume 1 - Introduction and Overview</u>. Publication G320-1370-0, June 1974.

_____. <u>Data Security and Data Processing, Volume 2 - Study Summary</u>. Publication G320-1371-0, June 1974.

_____. <u>Data Security and Data Processing, Volume 3 Part 1 - State of Illinois: Executive Overview</u>. Publication G320-1372-0, June 1974.

_____. <u>Data Security and Data Processing, Volume 3 Part 2 - Study Results: State of Illinois</u>. Publication G320-1373-0, June 1974, 428 pp.

_____. <u>Data Security and Data Processing, Volume 4 - Study Results: Massachusetts Institute of Technology</u>. Publication G320-1374-0, June 1974, 300 pp.

_____. <u>Data Security and Data Processing, Volume 5 - Study Results: TRW Systems, Inc</u>. Publication G320-1375-0, June 1974, 317 pp.

_____. <u>Data Security and Data Processing, Volume 6 - Evaluations and Installation Experiences: Resource Security System</u>. Publication G320-1376-0, June 1974.

_____. _IBM Data Security Forum - Denver, Colorado - September 1974_. Publication G520-2965-0, September 1974.

_____. _Computer-Assisted Job Placement in Corpus Christi, Texas_. Publication GK20-0886-0, August 1975, 14 pp.

_____. _Engineering Productivity with Interactive Computing at Rockwell International_. Publication GK20-0888-0, September 1975, 10 pp.

_____. _Computer-Assisted Instruction at the University of Akron_. Publication GK20-0818-0, April 1976, 13 pp.

_____. _Online Registration and Administration System at Palm Beach Junior College_. Publication GK20-0892-0, April 1976, 14 pp.

_____. _Online Analytical Lab System at Davison Chemical_. Publication GK20-0981-0, September 1976, 14 pp.

_____. _Innovative Computer Applications at the Crawford W. Long Memorial Hospital_. Publication GK20-1062-0, September 1977, 14 pp.

_____. _Data Secutity Through Cryptography_. Publication GC22-9062-0, October 1977, 32 pp.

_____. _Industrial Medical Support Systems Within IBM_. Publication GK20-1087-0, March 1978, 18 pp.

_____. _Computer-Assisted Electrocardiogram Analysis at Crouse Irving Memorial Hospital_. Publication GK20-1125-1, June 1978, 10 pp.

Immel, Richard A. "Whir, Click-Blooey: Sabotage, Accidents, and Fraud Woes for Computer Center." _Wall Street Journal_, 22 March 1971, p. 1.

"In Defense of Privacy." _Time_, 15 July 1966, pp. 38-39.

"Industry Looks Hard at Total Automation." _Industry Week_, vol. 193, no. 2, 25 April 1977, pp. 33, 36, 37.

Information. San Francisco, California: W.H. Freeman and Company, 1966, 218 pp. Also published as articles in _Scientific American_, September 1966.

Information Systems: Current Developments and Future Expansions. Montvale, New Jersey: AFIPS Press, 1970.

Information Technology: Some Critical Implications for Decision Makers. New York, New York: The Conference Board, Inc., Report 537, 1972.

Inman, Thomas H., and Krajewski, Lorrine. "A Futuristic View of Business Communication." _ABCA Bulletin_, vol. 41, no. 4, December 1978, pp. 15-17. Electronic communication.

Ishida, Harvisha, an interview with. "Personal Computing in Japan." Personal Computing, vol. 2, no. 3, March 1978, pp. 39-45.

Jackson, Carmault B., Jr. "Consideration on the 'Active Working Record' Versus the 'Permanent Record.'" Psychiatric Opinion, January 1975, pp. 29-33. The preliminary view of the American Society of Internal Medicine.

Jackson, Geoffrey G. "The Role of Administrators and Physicians in the Developement of Hospital Information Systems." Computers and Automation, vol. 19, no. 6, June 1970, pp. 33-35.

Jackson, Philip C., Jr. Introduction to Artificial Intelligence. New York, New York: Petrocelli/Charter, 1974, 453 pp.

Jaffe, Austin J. "Computer-Assisted Instruction and Real Estate Investment Analysis." The Real Estate Appraiser, vol. 42, no. 6, November-December 1976, pp. 21-28.

Jaki, Stanley L. Brain, Mind and Computer. New York, New York: Herder and Herder, 1969.

James, I.T. "Fraud and the Computer." Data Systems, July 1969, pp. 36-37.

James, Vaughn. "Integrating Reference Material into CAI." Journal of Systems Management, vol. 28, no. 12, December 1977, pp. 24-25.

Janda, Kenneth. Information Retrieval: Applications to Political Science. Indianapolis, Indiana: Bobbs-Merrill Company, 1968.

Jastrow, Robert. "Toward an Intelligence Beyond Man's." Time, vol. 11, no. 8, 20 February 1978, p. 59.

Jerman, Max. "Promising Developments in Computer-Assisted Instruction." Educational Technology, vol. 9, no. 4, April 1969, pp. 10-18.

_____. "Computers, Instruction, and the Curriculum." Educational Technology, vol. 10, no. 5, May 1970, pp. 53-56.

_____., and others. "A CAI Program for the Home." Educational Technology, vol. 11, no. 12, December 1971, p. 49.

Johansen, Robert; Vallee, Jacques; and Spangler, Kathleen. "Electronic Meetings: Utopian Dreams and Complex Realities." Futurist, vol. 12, no. 5, October 1978, pp. 313-319.

Johnson, C.B. "Protection Primer for EDP Records." Banking, December 1969, pp. 85-86.

Johnson, Robert J. "Computers in Education: An IBM Viewpoint." Educational Technology, vol. 11, no. 12, December 1971, pp. 16-18.

Jonas, Hans. "Technology and Responsibility: Reflections on the New Tasks of Ethics." Social Research, Spring 1973, pp. 31-54.

Jones, Charles P. "An Opportunity for Success." In Digest of Papers, pp. 123-124. New York, New York: The Institute of Electrical and Electronics Engineers, Inc., Spring COMPCON76, IEEE Catalog No. 76CH1069-4(CR), February 1976.

Jones, D.F. Colossus. New York, New York: G.P. Putnam's Sons, 1966. Science fiction.

_____. The Fall of Colossus. New York, New York: Berkley Medallion Books, 1974, 188 pp. Science fiction.

_____. Colossus and the Crab. New York, New York: Berkley Medallion Books, 1977, 219 pp. Science fiction.

Jones, P.F. "Four Principles of Man-Computer Dialog." IEEE Transactions on Professional Communication, vol. 21, no. 4, December 1978, pp. 154-159.

Jones, W.B. Computer: The Mind Stretcher. New York, New York: Dial Press, 1969.

Jones, William, and others. Approaches to Ethics: Representative Selection from Classic Times to the Present. New York, New York: McGraw-Hill Book Company, 1977.

Jonsen, Albert R., and Butler, Lewis H. "Public Ethics and Policy Making." Hastings Center Report, vol. 5, August 1975, pp. 19-31.

Jordan, James A., Jr. "Socratic Teaching?" Harvard Educational Review, vol. 33, 1963, pp. 96-104.

Joynt, John B. "Tradition and Change." Forum 70, vol. 2, no. 2, February 1970, pp. 8-11, 34, 36.

Judson, Horace Freeland. "Fearful of Science: Who Shall Watch the Scientists?" Harper's, June 1975, pp. 70-72, 74-76.

Jungk, Robert. Brighter than a Thousand Suns. New York, New York: Harcourt, 1958. Development of the atomic bomb.

Jungk, Robert, and Galtung, Johan, eds. Mankind 2000. London, England: George Allen and Unwin, Ltd., 1969.

"Junk Mail: Getting It - and Getting Rid of It." Consumer Reports, September 1976, pp. 540-542.

Jurgen, Ronald K., and Ernst, Martin L. "Electronic Funds Transfer: Too Much, Too Soon?" IEEE Spectrum, vol. 14, no. 5, May 1977, pp. 51-57.

Jutila, S.T., and Sass, C.J. "Uses of Computers for Corporate Strategy Development." Data Management, vol. 10, no. 9, September 1972, pp. 73-75.

Kagan, C.A.R.; Schear, L.G.; and Bernstein, G. "The Home Reckoner - A Scenario on the Home Use of Computers." AFIPS Conference Proceedings, vol. 42, 4-8 June 1973, pp. 759-763.

Kahn, D. The Codebreakers. New York, New York: The Macmillan Company, 1967, 1164 pp.

Kahn, Herman, and Wiener, Anthony J. The Year 2000: A Framework for Speculation on the Next Thirty-three Years. New York, New York: The Macmillan Company, 1967.

Kahn, Kenneth, and Lieberman, Henry. "Computer Animation: Snow White's Dream Machine." Technology Review, vol. 80, no. 1, October-November 1977, pp. 34-46.

Kaiser, Barbara L. "Patients' Rights of Access to Their Own Medical Records: The Need for New Law." Buffalo Law Review, Winter 1975, pp. 317-330.

Kalb, W.J. "Let User Decide Computer Use." Iron Age, vol. 200, 16 November 1967, pp. 54-55.

Kambic, George X., and Wake, Robert H. "Computed Tomography: The First Required Use of a Computer in Diagnostic Medicine." In Digest of Papers, pp. 306-310. New York, New York: The Institute of Electrical and Electronics Engineers, Inc., Fall COMPCON76, IEEE Catalog No. 76CH1115-5C, September 1976.

Kanal, Laveen N. "Interactive Pattern Analysis and Classification Systems: A Survey and Commentary." Proceedings of the IEEE, vol. 60, no. 10, October 1972, pp. 1200-1215.

Kaplan, Alan R. "Personal Computers: The Outlook for Home and Hobby Computers." Computer Decisions, vol. 9, no. 5, May 1977, pp. 36-40.

_____. "Home Computer Versus Hobby Computers." Datamation, vol. 23, no. 7, July 1977, pp. 72-75.

Kaplan, Louis, ed. Reader in Library Services and the Computer. Washington, D.C.: Microcard Editions, 1971, 239 pp.

Karbowiak, A.E., and Huey, R.M., eds. Information, Computers, Machines, and Man. New York, New York: John Wiley and Sons, 1971.

Karst, K.L. "The Files: Legal Controls Over the Accuracy and Accessibility of Stored Personal Data." Law and Contemporary Problems, vol. 31, Spring 1966, pp. 342, 376.

Katzan, Harry, Jr. Computer Data Security. New York, New York: Van Nostrand Reinhold Company, 1973.

_____. Information Technology: The Human Use of Computers. New York, New York: Petrocelli Books, 1974, 350 pp.

Katzenbach, Nicholas deB, and Tomic, Richard W. "Crime Data Centers: The Use of Computers in Crime Detection and Prevention." *Columbia Human Rights Law Review*, vol. 4, no. 1, Winter 1972, pp. 49-57.

Kaufman, Felix, and Johnston, Arch. "The Centralized Data Bank: An Alternative." *Government Data Systems*, May-June 1971, pp. 12-13, 39, 41.

Kaufmann, Carl B. "The Future Social Climate for R & D." *Research Management*, January 1975, pp. 29-32.

Kaysen, Carl. "Data Banks and Dossiers." *The Public Interest*, Spring 1967, pp. 52-60.

Keen, Peter G.W. "'Interactive' Computer Systems for Managers: A Modest Proposal." *Sloan Management Review*, vol. 18, no. 1, Fall 1976, pp. 1-17.

Kelleher, G.J. *The Challenge to System Analysis*. New York, New York: John Wiley and Sons, 1970.

Kelley, Clarence M. "White Collar Crime: The Strain on Our Economic System." *Management World*, vol. 6, no. 3, March 1977, pp. 34-36.

Kelley, Neil D. "No Computer is an Island." *Infosystems*, June 1978, pp. 3, 6-7. Product philosophy of Texas Instruments.

Kelly, Janice. "The Dossiers of American Citizens." *Computers and People*, vol. 24, no. 3, March 1975, pp. 16, 22-23, 28.

Kelly, W.E. "Computer Systems: Slaves or Masters?" *Management Accounting*, October 1971, pp. 9-11.

Kelman, H.C. "Human Use of Human Subjects: The Problem of Deception in Social Psychological Experiments." *Psychological Bulletin*, vol. 67, 1967, pp. 1-11.

Kemeny, John G. *Man and the Computer*. New York, New York: Charles Scribner's Sons, 1972, 151 pp.

Keplinger, Michael. "The Copyright Law, Higher Education and Technological Change." *Computers and Society*, vol. 8, no. 3, Fall 1977, pp. 7-10.

Kershaw, J.A., and McKean, R.N. "Systems Analysis and Education." Santa Monica, California: The RAND Corporation, Report RM-2473-FF, 30 October 1959, 64 pp.

Kershner, Howard E. "Why Civilizations Rise and Fall: Ethics and Money." *Vital Speeches of the Day*, 15 January 1974, pp. 216-221.

Kiersh, Ed. "More Grief for States-Bound Smugglers." *High Times*, no. 28, December 1977, p. 48. Treasury Enforcement Communications Systems (TECS).

Kiester, Sally Valente. "It's Student and Computer, One on One." *Change*, vol. 10, January 1978, pp. 56-58.

King, Jack H. "The 'Free Resource' and the Junior College." *Educational Technology*, vol. 10, no. 3, March 1970, pp. 24-27.

King, William R. "Intelligent MIS - A Management Helper." *Business Horizons*, vol. 16, no. 5, October 1973, pp. 5-12.

Kintisch, Robert S. "It's Still a Big Step to Install a Small Computer." *Administrative Management*, vol. 39, no. 11, November 1978, pp. 26-29, 45.

Kintisch, Ronald S., and Weisbord, Marvin R. "Getting Computer People and Users to Understand Each Other." *Advanced Management Journal*, vol. 42, no. 2, Spring 1977, pp. 4-14.

Kirchner, Jake. "GAO Labels Federal DP Security 'Inadequate.'" *Computerworld*, vol. 12, no. 47, 20 November 1978, p. 12.

Kirkpatrick, L. Duane. "Future Computer Systems." New York, New York: G.A. Saxton and Company, Inc., Industry Notes No. 33, 26 March 1973, 18 pp. Based on Madnick's report, February 1973.

Klein, Marjorie H.; Greist, John H.; and Van Cura, Lawrence J. "Computers and Psychiatry: Promises to Keep." *Archives of General Psychiatry*, vol. 32, July 1975, pp. 837-843.

Kleinschrod, Walter A. "The Privacy Issue: Big Brother or Big Bother?" *Administrative Management*, vol. 37, no. 8, August 1976, p. 23.

Kling, Rob. "Computers and Social Power." *Computers and Society*, Fall 1974, pp. 6-11.

_____. "EFTS: Social and Technical Issues - What Are EFTS?" *Computers and Society*, vol. 7, no. 3, Fall 1976, pp. 3-10.

_____. "Value Conflicts and Social Choice in Electronic Funds Transfer System Developments." *Communications of the ACM*, vol. 21, no. 8, August 1978, pp. 642-657.

Knight, Lucy. "Facts about Mr. Buckley's Amendment." *American Education*, vol. 13, no. 5, June 1977, pp. 6-9. The law's relevancy to school districts.

Knight, Robert E. "The Changing Payments Mechanism: Electronic Funds Transfer Arrangements." *Monthly Review*, July-August 1974, pp. 10-20.

Kochen, Manfred, ed. *The Growth of Knowledge: Readings on Organization and Retrieval of Information*. New York, New York: John Wiley and Sons, 1967.

Kochenburger, Ralph J., and Turcio, Carolyn J. *Computers in Modern Society*. New York, New York: John Wiley and Sons, 1974.

Koehn, Hank E. "Are Companies Bugged About Bugging?" *Journal of Systems Management*, January 1973, pp. 12-13.

Kolata, Gina Bari. "The End of Elegance: The Computer Invades Mathematics." *The Sciences*, vol. 17, no. 3, May-June 1977, pp. 6-9.

Koller, William. *Your Career in Computer-Related Occupations*. New York, New York: Arco Publishing Company, Inc., 1978.

Kooi, Beverly Y., and Geddes, Cleone. "The Teacher's Role in Computer-Assisted Instructional Management." *Educational Technology*, vol. 10, no. 2, February 1970, pp. 42-45.

Kopstein, F.F. "Why CAI Must Fail!" *Educational Technology*, vol. 10, no. 3, March 1970, pp. 51-53.

Kozdrowicki, Edward W., and Cooper, Dennis W. "When Will a Computer be World Chess Champion?" *Computer Decisions*, vol. 6, no. 8, August 1974, pp. 28-30, 32.

Kozmetsky, George, and Kircher, P. *Electronic Computers and Management Control*. New York, New York: McGraw-Hill Book Company, 1956.

Kozmetsky, George, and Ruefli, Timothy W. *Information Technology: Initiatives for Today, Decisions that Cannot Wait*. Edited by DuBois S. Morris, Jr. New York, New York: The Conference Board, Inc., Report 577, 1972, 50 pp.

Kraemer, Kenneth L. "Local Government, Information Systems, and Technology Transfer: Evaluating Some Common Assertions about Computer Application Transfer." *Public Administration Review*, vol. 37, no. 4, July-August 1977, pp. 368-382.

Kraemer, Kenneth L.; King, John Leslie; and Colton, Kent. "Towards an Agenda for EFT Research." *Computers and Society*, vol. 8, no. 2, Summer 1977, pp. 3-11.

Kraemer, Kenneth L., and Mitchel, William H. "Urban Data Processing." *Datamation*, vol. 13, no. 8, August 1967, pp. 66-68.

Kraemer, Kenneth L., and Whisenand, Paul M. "Status of Automatic Data Processing in Los Angeles and Orange Counties." *Data Processing Magazine*, June 1966, pp. 28-33.

Kranz, Stewart. *Science and Technology in the Arts*. New York, New York: Van Nostrand Reinhold Company, 1974.

Kranzberg, M. "Computers: New Values for Society." *Management Review*, vol. 56, February 1967, pp. 30-33.

Krendel, Ezia S. "A Case Study of Citizen Complaints as Social Indicators." *IEEE Transactions on Systems Science and Cybernetics*, October 1970, pp. 265-272.

Krumboltz, John D., and Weisman, Ronald G. "The Effect of Overt Versus Convert Responding to Programed Instruction on Immediate and Delated Retention." *Journal of Educational Psychology*, vol. 53, no. 2, 1962, pp. 89-92.

Kuch, Terry D.C., and others. "Computers and Elections." *Computers and Society*, Summer 1976, pp. 3-7.

_____. "Computers and Elections II." *Computers and Society*, Fall 1976, p. 15.

Kugel, Peter. "The Controversy Goes On - 'Can Computers Think?' Part I: Background." *Creative Computing*, vol. 5, no. 8, August 1979, pp. 46-50.

_____. "The Controversy Goes On - 'Can Computers Think?' Part II: What is Thinking?" *Creative Computing*, vol. 5, no. 9, September 1979, pp. 104-109.

Kuhfeld, Albert H. "Spacewar." *Analog*, vol. 87, no. 5, July 1971, pp. 67-79.

Kuong, Javier F. *Computer Security, Auditing and Controls: A Bibliography*. Wellesley Hills, Massachusetts: Management Advisory Press, 1973.

Kurland, Philip B. "The Private I: Some Reflections on Privacy and the Constitution." *State Government*, Winter 1977, pp. 12-15.

Kutnick, Dale. "Distributed Processing and the Automated Office." *The Office*, vol. 88, no. 3, September 1978, pp. 143-144, 146, 157.

Laird, Donald A., and Laird, E.C.L. *How to Get Along with Automation*. New York, New York: McGraw-Hill Book Company, 1963.

Lakoff, Stanford A., ed. *Knowledge and Power: Essays on Science and Government*. New York, New York: The Free Press, 1966, 502 pp.

Lambert, Roy. "The Next Hundred Years: A Course." *Computers and Society*, Summer 1974, pp. 5-8.

Lamond, Fred. "Europeans Blame Computers." *Datamation*, vol. 24, no. 11, November 1978, pp. 107, 110, 114.

Lane, Robert E. "The Decline of Politics and Ideology in a Knowledgeable Society." *American Sociological Review*, October 1966, pp. 649-662.

Langer, Richard W. "Home Computers: Here Today, Everywhere Tomorrow." *ROM*, July 1977, pp. 26-32.

La Porte, Todd R., and Metlay, Daniel. "Technology Observed: Attitude of a Wary Public." *Science*, vol. 188, 11 April 1975, pp. 121-127.

Lapp, Ralph E. *The New Priesthood: The Scientific Elite and the Uses of Power*. New York, New York: Harper and Row, 1965, 244 pp.

Laska, Richard M. "The World Model Controversy: Will Mankind Survive?" *Computer Decisions*, vol. 4, no. 4, April 1972, pp. 24-27.

_____. "All the News That's Fit to Retrieve." *Computer Decisions*, vol. 4, no. 8, August 1972, pp. 18-22.

Lasswell, Harold D. "Do We Need Social Observatories?" *Saturday Review*, 5 August 1967, pp. 49-52.

Lasswell, Harold D., and Kaplan, Abraham. *Power and Society*. New Haven, Connecticut: Yale University Press, 1950.

Laudon, Kenneth C. *Computers and Bureaucratic Reform*. New York, New York: John Wiley and Sons, 1974.

Lautenberg, Frank R. "Computing Services: Industry or Coincidence?" *Computers and People*, vol. 27, nos. 11-12, November-December 1978, pp. 8, 12, 21.

Lautsch, John C. "Foundations of Various State Information Practices Laws." *Data Management*, January 1977, pp. 19-23.

Lavendel, Giuliana A. "The Computer in Research: A Real-Time Partner." *IEEE Spectrum*, vol. 15, no. 12, December 1978, pp. 38-40.

Laver, F.J.M. "Computers and Society." In *Processings of the Joint IBM University of Newcastle upon Tyne Seminar*, pp. 91-120. Newcastle, England: University of Newcastle upon Tyne, 9-12 September 1975.

Laver, Murray. *Computers, Communications, and Society*. New York, New York: Oxford University Press, Inc., 1975.

Lavington, S.H. *A History of Manchester Computers*. Manchester, England: NCC Publications, 1975.

Layton, E.T., Jr. *The Revolt of the Engineers, Social Responsibility and the American Engineering Profession*. Cleveland, Ohio: Case Western Reserve, 1971.

_____. "Engineering Ethics and the Public Interest: A Historical View." New York, New York: The American Society of Mechanical Engineers, Publication 76-WA/TS-9, December 1976.

Leaver, E.W., and Brown, J.J. "Electronics and Human Beings." *Harper's*, August 1951, pp. 88-93.

Leavitt, Ruth, ed. *Artist and Computer*. New York, New York: Harmony Books, 1976.

Lederberg, Joshua. "The Freedoms and the Control of Science: Notes From the Ivory Tower." *Southern California Law Review*, Spring 1972, pp. 596-614.

Ledley, Robert S. *Use of Computer in Biology and Medicine*. New York, New York: McGraw-Hill Book Company, 1965.

Lee, H.C. "Organizational Impact of Computers." *Management Services*, vol. 4, May 1967, pp. 39-43.

Lee, John F. "Clearing House Interbank Payments System." *Computers and Society*, vol. 7, no. 4, Winter 1976, pp. 6-9.

Lee, Robert S. "The Computer's Public Image." *Datamation*, vol. 12, no. 12, December 1966, pp. 33-34, 39.

_____. "Social Attitudes and the Computer Revolution." *Public Opinion Quarterly*, vol. 34, no. 1, Spring 1970, pp. 53-59.

Leed, Jacob. *The Computer and Literacy Style*. Kent, Ohio: Kent State University Press, 1968.

Lees, John. "An Esoteric Ethical Excursion." *Creative Computing*, March-April 1976, p. 33.

Lehman, Todd. "Computers for Business Use." *Administrative Management*, vol. 30, no. 11, November 1969, pp. 53-60.

Lekan, Helen. *Index of Computer-Assisted Instruction*. New York, New York: Harcourt Brace Jovanovich, 1972.

Leibholz, S.W., and Wilson, L.D. *User's Guide to Computer Crime: It's Commission, Detection, and Prevention*. Radnor, Pennsylvania: Chilton Book Company, 1974.

Lein, Harry. "Detecting Fire 'Thief' Prime Security Concern." *Data Management*, May 1977, pp. 26-27.

Leininger, Joseph E., and Gilchrist, Bruce, eds. *Computers, Society and Law: The Role of Legal Education*. Montvale, New Jersey: AFIPS Press, 1973.

Lem, Stanislaw. *The Cyberiad: Fables for the Cybernetic Age*. New York, New York: Avon Books, 1974. Science fiction.

Lennon, Richard E. "Cryptography Architecture for Information Security." *IBM Systems Journal*, vol. 17, no. 2, 1978, pp. 138-150.

Leonard, Donald C. "Banking and Consumer-Oriented POS/EFTS." In *Computer Technology to Reach the People: Digest of Papers*, pp. 163-166. New York, New York: The Institute of Electrical and Electronics Engineers, Inc., Spring COMPCON75, IEEE Catalog No. 75CH0920-9C, February 1975.

Lester, Tom. "The Office Conundrum." *Management Today*, November 1978, pp. 116-117, 120, 122, 124.

Levi, Albert W. _Philosophy and the Modern World_. Bloomington, Indiana: Indiana University Press, 1959.

Levien, Roger E., ed. _The Emerging Technology: Instructional Uses of the Computer in Higher Education_. New York, New York: McGraw-Hill Book Company, 1972.

Levinson, Robert E. "How to Conquer the Panic of Change." _Management Review_, vol. 66, no. 7, July 1977, pp. 20-24.

Lewinsohn, Richard. _Science, Prophecy, and Prediction_. New York, New York: Harper and Row, Publishers, 1961.

Lewis, Arthur O., Jr. _Of Men and Machines_. New York, New York: E.P. Dutton and Company, 1963. Anthology of short stories, essays, and poems.

Lewis, David A. "Computerized Assistance for the Aging." _Journal of Systems Management_, vol. 22, no. 4, April 1971, pp. 21-43.

Lewis, Theodore G. _How to Profit from Your Personal Computer: Professional, Business, and Home Applications_. Rochelle Park, New Jersey: Hayden Book Company, Inc., 1978.

_____. _The Mind Appliance: Home Computer Applications_. Rochelle Park, New Jersey: Hayden Book Company, Inc., 1978, 138 pp.

Lewis, Theodore G., and Shriver, Bruce D., eds. "The Oregon Report: Blueprint Papers from the Conference on Computing in the 1980's." Special issue of _Computer_, vol. 11, no. 9. September 1978.

Lewis, Thomas L. "The Selection and Installation of a Computer-Based Hospital Information System." In _Digest of Papers_, pp. 315-317. New York, New York: The Institute of Electrical and Electronics Engineers, Inc., Fall COMPCON76, IEEE Catalog No. 76CH1115-5C, September 1976.

Licklider, J.C.R. _Libraries of the Future_. Cambridge, Massachusetts: MIT Press, 1965.

Licklider, J.C.R., and Vezza, Albert. "Applications of Information Networks." _Proceedings of the IEEE_, vol. 66, no. 11, November 1978, pp. 1330-1346.

Lickson, Charles P. "Privacy and the Computer Age." _IEEE Spectrum_, vol. 5, no. 10, October 1968, pp. 58-63.

Lieberman, Jethro K. "How Much Government?" _The Center Magazine_, May-June 1977, pp. 63-77.

Lien, Ronald L. "Appropriate Use of the Computer for Instructional Purposes." _Educational Technology_, vol. 14, no. 12, December 1974, pp. 35-39.

Lincoln, Harry B., ed. _The Computer and Music_. Ithaca, New York: Cornell University Press, 1970.

_____. "The Current State of Music Research and the Computer." Computers and the Humanities, vol. 5, no. 1, September 1970, pp. 29-36.

Lindberg, Donald A.B. The Computer and Medical Care. Springfield, Illinois: Charles C. Thomas, Publisher, 1968.

Lindsay, P.H., and Norman, D.A. Human Information Processing. New York, New York: Academic Press, 1972.

Link, Mary. "Medical Records Aren't So Secret." The Times-Picayune, Section 1, 4 September 1977, p. 35.

Linowes, David F. "Are New Privacy Laws Needed?" Vital Speeches of the Day, vol. 44, no. 14, 1 May 1978, pp. 436-439.

_____. "How Databanks Get the Goods on Everybody." Business and Social Review, no. 26, Summer 1978, pp. 54-57.

Lipis, Allen H. "Electronic Funds Transfer Helps Banks Fight Check Deluge." Computer Decisions, vol. 4, no. 11, November 1972, pp. 18-22.

Lobel, Jerome. "Computer Privacy States' Side: Seeking Cooperation Amid Confusion." Data Management, vol. 15, no. 4, April 1977, pp. 12-15, 55.

Lodge, George Cabot. "Ethics and the New Ideology: Can Business Adjust." Management Review, vol. 66, no. 7, July 1977, pp. 10-19.

Logsdon, Tom. The Computers in Our Society. Fullerton, California: Anaheim Publishing Company, 1974.

Lonergan, Gerald J., and Ryan, E. "A Review of an Employee Information System." Internal Auditor, vol. 34, no. 2, April 1977, pp. 80-82.

Long, H.S.; O'Neal, L.R.; and Schwartz, H.A. "Exploratory Results from the Application of Computer-Assisted Instruction to Industrial Training." Poughkeepsie, New York: IBM Corporation, Technical Report 00.1790, January 1969, 29 pp.

"Long Wait." Time, 16 October 1978, p. 96. Use of the Universal Product Code.

Lorber, Michael A. "Increased Learning Freedom Via Computers." Educational Technology, vol. 14, no. 2, February 1974, pp. 44-47.

Lord, Kenniston W., Jr. "Data Center Security: A Case for the Private Eye." Infosystems, vol. 23, no. 12, December 1976, pp. 30-33.

Losty, P.A. The Effective Use of Computers in Business. London, England: Cassell and Company, Ltd., 1969.

Lottes, James F. "The Georgia Urban Information System." *Law and Computer Technology*, August 1969, pp. 10-13.

Loughary, John. *Man-Machine Systems in Education*. New York, New York: Harper and Row, Publishers, 1966.

Lowry, Robert A. "Watch Out: Those Built-in Computers Will Get You." *Management Review*, vol. 66, no. 1, January 1977, pp. 12-17.

Luehrmann, Arthur W. "Should the Computer Teach the Student, or Vice-Versa?" *Creative Computing*, vol. 2, no. 6, November-December 1976, pp. 42-45.

Lumsdaine, A.A. "Teaching Machines and Self-Instructional Materials." *Audio-Visual Communication Review*, vol. 7, 1959, pp. 163-181.

Lundell, E. Drake, Jr. "Disclosure of Federal Dossires Proposed." *Computerworld*, vol. 6, 28 June 1972, p. 1.

_____. "No Argument - 'DP Causes Unemployment.'" *Computerworld*, vol. 11, no. 34, 22 August 1977, pp. 1, 6.

_____. "Sociologist - Computers Widening 'Power Gap.'" *Computerworld*, vol. 11, no. 37, 12 September 1977, p. 9.

Luria, S.E. "Conformity vs. Concern." *Hastings Center Report*, April 1976, p. 4.

Lykos, Peter. "Computer Myths Live in 1975." *Computers and Society*, Winter 1975, pp. 5-6.

MacBride, Robert O. *The Automated State: Computer Systems as a New Force in Society*. Philadephia, Pennsylvania: Chilton Book Company, 1967, 407 pp.

MacGuffie, J.V. "Computer Programs for People." *Personnel Journal*, vol. 48, April 1969, pp. 253-258.

Macklin, Ruth. "Moral Concerns and Appeals to Rights and Duties." *Hastings Center Report*, October 1976, pp. 31-38.

Macmillan, R.H. *Automation: Friend or Foe?* New York, New York: Cambridge University Press, 1956.

Macrae, N. "Toward the Age of No Experience: Where the Computer Revolution Should Lead Us." *Economist*, vol. 242, 22 January 1972, pp. 9-10.

Macrae, Norman. "How to Survive in the Age of Telecommuting." *Management Review*, vol. 67, no. 11, November 1978, pp. 14-19.

Madgwick, D., and Smythe, T. *The Invasion of Privacy*. Brooklyn Heights, New York: Beekman Publishers, Inc., 1974.

Madnick, Stuart E. "Recent Technical Advances in the Computer Industry and Their Future Impact." Cambridge, Massachusetts: Massachusetts Institute of Technology, Industrial Liaison Program Report 645-73, February 1973, 29 pp.

_____. "Trends in Computers and Computing: The Information Utility." *Science*, vol. 195, no. 4283, 18 March 1977, pp. 1191-1199.

Mager, Robert F. "Preliminary Studies in Automated Teaching." *IRE Transactions on Education*, vol. 2, June 1959, pp. 104-107.

"Magnetic Larceny." *Modern Data*, October 1973, p. 31.

Makower, J. "Plastic Fantastic Money." *Politics Today*, vol. 5, July 1978, pp. 57-58.

Malde, Bharat. "The Human Intermediary in the Use of Computers." *Computers and People*, vol. 26, no. 2, February 1977, pp. 22-23.

Malik, Rex. "Britons Fearful of DP." *Computerworld*, vol. 12, no. 41, 9 October 1978, pp. 1, 8.

Mallary, R. "Computer Sculpture: Six Levels of Cybernetics." *Artforum*, May 1969, pp. 29-35. Impact of computers on art.

Mallinson, C.W. "The Use of Computers in Local Government in Great Britain." *Law and Computer Technology*, August 1969, pp. 16-23.

Maloney, James V., Jr. "Computers: The Physical Sciences and Medicine." *AFIPS Conference Proceedings*, FJCC, vol. 27, Part 2, November-December 1965, pp. 17-19.

Mandell, Mel. "Computer-Based Planning: The Once and Future Thing." *Computer Decisions*, vol. 11, no. 6, June 1979, pp. 38-39, 42.

Mandell, Steven L. "The Management Information System is Going to Pieces." *California Management Review*, Summer 1975, pp. 50-56.

Maniotes, John, and Quasney, James. *Computer Careers: Planning, Prerequisites, Potential*. Rochelle Park, New Jersey: Hayden Book Company, 1974.

Mantell, Murray I. *Ethics and Professionalism in Engineering*. New York, New York: The Macmillan Company, 1964.

Marcuse, Herbert. "Remarks on a Redefinition of Culture." *Daedalus*, vol. 94, no. 1, Winter 1965, pp. 190-207.

Margolin, Joseph B., and Misch, Marion R., eds. *Computers in the Classroom*. Rochelle Park, New Jersey: Hayden Book Company, 1970, 382 pp.

Marks, C.P. "The Impact on the User of the Microcomputer Revolution." *Management Services in Government*, vol. 33, no. 4, November 1978, pp. 177-184.

Marois, M. *Man and Computer*. New York, New York: Elsevier-North Holland Publishing Company, 1975.

Maron, M.E. "Design Principles for an Intelligent Machine." Santa Monica, California: The RAND Corporation, Report P-2572, March 1962, 25 pp.

Marschak, Alexander. *The Roots of Civilization*. New York, New York: The Macmillan Company, 1972.

Marshall, J. "Big D by Three." *Sports Illustrated*, vol. 49, 4 September 1978, pp. 34-35. Computers used to help predict outcomes of professional football games.

Martin, J.J., and others. "Panel: Certification and Licensing." *Data Management*, vol. 15, no. 1, January 1977, pp. 31-37.

Martin, James. *Security, Accuracy, and Privacy in Computer Systems*. Englewood Cliffs, New Jersey: Prentice-Hall, Inc., 1973, 626 pp.

Martin, James, and Norman, Adrian R.D. *The Computerized Society*. Englewood Cliffs, New Jersey: Prentice-Hall, Inc., 1970, 560 pp.

Martin, Peter. "An Appropriate Management Information System for a Kingdom." *Computers and People*, vol. 25, no. 12, December 1976, pp. 14-15, 18.

Marx, Otto M. "A Warning from the Historian." *Psychiatric Opinion*, February 1975, pp. 34-35. The problem of some proposals on confidentiality of health records.

Mason, E.E., and Bulgren, W.C. *Computer Applications in Medicine*. Springfield, Illinois: Charles Thomas, Publisher, 1964.

Matheson, Willard E. "The Brain and the Machine." *Personal Computing*, vol. 2, no. 4, April 1978, pp. 37-45.

Mathews, Max V. "The Computer as a Musical Instrument." *Computer Decisions*, vol. 4, no. 2, February 1972, pp. 22-25.

Mathison, S.L., and Walker, P.M. *Computers and Telecommunications: Issues in Public Policy*. Englewood Cliffs, New Jersey: Prentice-Hall, Inc., 1969.

Matusow, H. *The Beast of Business: A Record of Computer Atrocities*. London, England: Wolfe Publishing Ltd., 1968.

Maul, A.B. "Computer Development in the West Indies." *Computer Bulletin*, July 1969, pp. 224-227.

Maxwell, Neil. "Voice of Experience: Lamer Hill, Embezzler, Says Stealing is Easy." *Wall Street Journal*, 26 January 1973, p. 1.

May, Richard E. "The Use of the Computer in Schools." *Independent School Bulletin*, vol. 30, no. 4, May 1971, pp. 47-49.

Mazlack, Lawrence J. "Developing Computer Awareness." SIGCSE Bulletin, vol. 9, no. 1, February 1977, pp. 184-187.

Mazlish, Bruce. "The Fourth Discontinuity." Technology and Culture, January 1967, pp. 1-15.

M'Bow, Amadou Mahtar. "Wisdom Not Fate Will Be the Determiner in Information Handling." Computers and People, vol. 28, nos. 5-6, May-June 1979, pp. 8-12.

McBrier, C. Robert. "Impact of Computers on Retailing." AFIPS Conference Proceedings, FJCC, vol. 27, Part 2, November-December 1965, pp. 21-25.

McCarn, D.B., and Leiter, J. "On-Line Services in Medicine and Beyond." Science, vol. 181, 1973, pp. 318-324.

McCartney, Laton. "Users Drive Harder Bargains." Dun's Review, vol. 112, no. 1, July 1978, pp. 77, 80, 82, 85, 88. Negotiating for computers.

McCauley, C.S. Computers and Creativity, New York, New York: Praeger, 1974.

McClintock, Robert. "Machines and Vitalists: Reflections on the Ideology of Cybernetics." American Scholar, Spring 1966, pp. 249-257.

McCracken, Daniel D. Public Policy and the Expert. New York, New York: Council on Religion and International Affairs, 1971.

_____. "A Problem-List of Issues Concerning Computer and Public Policy." Communications of the ACM, vol. 17, no. 9, September 1974, pp. 495-503.

_____. "Will an Electronic Funds Transfer Network be in the Public's Interest." Data Communications, vol. 6, no. 4, April 1977, pp. 59-64.

McCracken, Paul W. "What Our Society Should Be All About." Across the Board, July 1977, pp. 4-10.

McDaniel, Herman. Career in Computers and Data Processing. Princeton, New Jersey: PBI-Petrocelli Books, 1978.

McDermott, John. "Technology: The Opiate of the Intellectuals." New York Review of Books, vol. 13, 31 July 1969, pp. 25-35.

McKay, William. "Computer-Directed Instructional Games." Audio-Visual Instruction, vol. 14, no. 4, April 1969, pp. 37-40.

McKnight, Gerald. Computer Crime. New York, New York: Walker and Company, 1973.

_____. Computer Crime: How a New Breed of Criminals is Making Off with Millions. London, England: Michael Joseph, 1974.

McLagan, Patricia A., and Sandborgh, Raymond E. "Computer-Aided Instruction: What It Is - What It Will Cost You." *Training*, vol. 14, no. 9, September 1977, pp. 48-50.

_____. "Computer-Aided Instruction: How to Get Started." *Training*, vol. 14, no. 9, September 1977, pp. 51-52.

_____. "Computer-Aided Instruction: Who's in Control Here?" *Training*, vol. 14, no. 9, September 1977, pp. 54-55.

McLaughlin, R.A. "Equity Funding: Everyone is Pointing at the Computer." *Datamation*, vol. 19, no. 6, June 1973, pp. 88-89, 91.

_____. "The (Mis)Use of DP in Government Agencies." *Datamation*, vol. 24, no. 7, July 1978, pp. 147-148, 150-151, 154, 156-157.

McLuhan, Marshall. *Understanding Media*. New York, New York: McGraw-Hill Book Company, 1964.

McLuhan, Marshall, and Watson, W. *From Cliche to Archetype*. New York, New York: Viking Press, Inc., 1970.

McNiven, J.D. "Bureaucratic Imperatives and Citizen Access: Some Theoretical Possibilities." *Optimum*, vol. 7, no. 3, 1976, pp. 22-33.

McRainey, John H. "Understanding CAM - Its Pitfalls and Promises." *Automation*, April 1975, pp. 58-63.

Meadows, Donella H., and others. *The Limits to Growth*. 2nd edition. New York, New York: Universe Books, 1974.

Meek, B.L., and Fairthorne, S. *Using Computers*. New York, New York: Halsted Press, 1977.

Megginson, Leon C. "The Human Consequences of Office Automation." *Personnel*, vol. 37, September-October 1960, pp. 18-26.

Meissner, Paul. "The Sensuous Computer - Gaining Access to Systems Through Touch, Voice, Signature and Other Personal Methods." *Data Management*, vol. 15, no. 5, May 1977, pp. 23-25.

Meltzer, B., ed. *Machine Intelligence*. New York, New York: American Elsevier, 1969.

Mendel, Arthur P. "Robots and Rebels." *New Republic*, 11 January 1969, pp. 16-19.

Menkus, Belden. "Computer and Management." *Administrative Management*, vol. 37, no. 5, May 1977, p. 118.

Merkin, William I., and Long, Raymond J. "The Application of Computers to Domestic and International Trade." *AFIPS Conference Proceedings*, FJCC, vol. 27, Part 2, November-December 1965, pp. 27-31.

Mesarovic, Mihajlo, and Pestel, Eduard. Mankind at the Turning Point - The Second Report to The Club of Rome. New York, New York: E.P. Dutton and Company, Inc./Reader's Digest Press, 1974.

Messier, Claire V. "A Computerized Electronic Mail System." The Office, vol. 88, no. 5, November 1978, pp. 82, 84, 87.

Mesthene, Emmanuel G. "How Technology Will Shape the Future." Science, vol. 161, 12 July 1968, pp. 135-143.

———. "Technology and Humanistic Values." Computers and the Humanities, vol. 4, no. 1, September 1969, pp. 1-10.

———. Technological Change: Its Impact on Man and Society. Cambridge, Massachusetts: Harvard University Press, 1970.

Meyer, Herbert E. "A Computer May be Deciding What You Get Paid." Fortune, November 1973, pp. 168-172, 176.

Meyer, Marshall W. "Automation and Bureaucratic Structure." American Journal of Sociology, November 1968, pp. 256-264.

Michael, Donald N. Cybernation: The Silent Conquest. Santa Barbara, California: Center for the Study of Democratic Institutions, 1962, 48 pp.

———. "Speculations on the Relation of the Computer to Individual Freedom and the Right to Privacy." George Washington Law Review, vol. 33, October 1964, pp. 270-286.

———. "Some Long-Range Implications of Computer Technology for Human Behavior in Organizations." American Behavioral Scientist, April 1966, pp. 29-35.

———. "Social Engineering and the Future Environment." American Psychologist, November 1967, pp. 588-592.

———. The Unprepared Society: Planning for a Precarious Future. New York, New York: Basic Books, Inc., 1968.

———. "Planning and Politics." Daedalus, vol. 97, Fall 1968, pp. 1179-1193.

Mikelsons, M. "Computer-Assisted Application Description." Yorktown Heights, New York: IBM Corporation, Report RC-5387, November 1974, 34 pp.

Miller, Arthur R. "Personal Privacy in the Computer Age: The Challenge of a New Technology in an Information-Oriented Society." Michigan Law Review, vol. 67, April 1969, pp. 1091-1246.

———. "Psychological Testing: Can We Minimize the Perils." Think, vol. 35, May-June 1969, pp. 24-26.

———. The Assault on Privacy: Computers, Data Banks, and Dossiers. Ann Arbor, Michigan: University of Michigan Press, 1971, 333 pp.

_____. "The Dossier Society." *University of Illinois Law Forum*, vol. 2, 1971, pp. 154-167.

_____. "Federal Data Banks and the Bill of Rights." *Computers and Automation*, October 1971, pp. 12-18.

_____. "The Assault on Privacy." *Psychiatric Opinion*, vol. 12, no. 1, January 1975, pp. 6-14.

Miller, Frederick W. "Psssst...Here Comes Personal Computing." *Infosystems*, vol. 25, no. 4, April 1978, pp. 54-55, 58.

_____. "A 'Common Sense' Approach Pays Off." *Infosystems*, vol. 25, no. 8, August 1978, pp. 39-42, 46. Data security.

_____. "The Postal Person Disappeareth." *Infosystems*, vol. 25, no. 12, December 1978, pp. 35, 38-39. Electronic mail.

Miller, George A. "Thinking Machines: Myths and Actualities." *The Public Interest*, Winter 1966, pp. 92-97, 99-108.

Miller, R.B. "Response Time in Man-Computer Conversational Transactions." Poughkeepsie, New York: IBM Corporation, Technical Report 00.1660, January 1968, 21 pp.

_____. "System Strategy in Human Factors." Poughkeepsie, New York: IBM Corporation, Report AR-0932-00, February 1968, 7 pp.

Miller, Robert J. "Can EDP Win the War on Crime?" *Datamation*, vol. 14, no. 6, June 1968, pp. 81-84.

Miller, W.E. "The Impact of Digital Computers Upon Steal Works Operations." *Computers and Automation*, vol. 17, no. 7, July 1968, pp. 22-25.

Miller, William B. "How to Make the EDP Function More Effective." *Management Review*, April 1977, pp. 18-27.

Milliman, Gordon. "Alameda County's 'People Information System.'" *Datamation*, vol. 13, no. 3, March 1967, pp. 28-31.

Mills, C. Wright. *The Power Elite*. New York, New York: Oxford University Press, 1956.

Minsky, Marvin L. "Steps Toward Artificial Intelligence." *Proceedings of the IRE*, vol. 49, January 1961, pp. 8-30.

_____. "I Think, Therefore I Am." *Psychology Today*, vol. 2, no. 11, April 1969, pp. 30-32.

Mitcham, Carl, and Mackey, Robert, eds. *Philosophy and Technology: Readings in the Philosophical Problems of Technology*. New York, New York: The Free Press, 1972.

Mitchell, George W. "Effects of Automation on the Structure and Functioning of Banking." *Journal of Accountancy*, vol. 121, no. 3, March 1966, pp. 60-61.

Mitchell, J.L., ed. Computers in the Humanities. Minneapolis, Minnesota: University of Minnesota Press, 1974.

Mitroff, Ian I.; Nelson, John; and Mason, Richard O. "On Management Myth-Information Systems." Management Science, vol. 21, no. 4, December 1974, pp. 371-382.

Mitzel, Harold E. "Computers and Adaptive Education." American Education, vol. 6, no. 10, December 1970, pp. 23-26.

Mizelle, W.R. "Automation: A Union Gray Train?" Antioch Review, vol. 18, Spring 1958, pp. 87-90.

Modesitt, Kenneth L. "Cooperative Efforts in Individualized Education." Computers and Society, vol. 8, no. 2, Summer 1977, pp. 12-14.

Molnar, Andrew R. "Critical Issues in Computer-Based Learning." Educational Technology, vol. 11, no. 8, August 1971, pp. 60-64.

Moncreiff, B., and Fumino, M.A. "A Fully Automated Computer-Managed Instruction System." Los Gatos, California: IBM Corporation, Report 16.190, February 1970, 31 pp.

Montague, A., and Snyder, S.S. Man and the Computer. New York, New York: Mason/Charter, 1972.

Moorer, James Anderson. "Music and Computer Composition." Communications of the ACM, vol. 15, no. 2, February 1972, pp. 104-113.

Morgan, Dan. "The District Government on Tape." Potomac Magazine, 1 January 1967, pp. 12-15.

Morgan, Howard L., and Soden, John V. "Understanding MIS Failures." Data Base, vol. 5, nos. 2-4, Winter 1973, pp. 157-171.

Morgenthau, Hans J. Science: Servant or Master? New York, New York: New American Library, 1972.

Morrill, Charles S. "Computer-Aided Instruction as Part of a Management Information System." Human Factors, vol. 9, no. 3, 1967, pp. 251-256.

Morris, Martin A. "Licensing? - Who Needs It!" Infosystems, April 1975, pp. 46-47.

Morris, Robert. "The Data Encryption Standard: Retrospective and Prospects." Communications, vol. 16, no. 6, November 1978, pp. 11-14.

Morrison, H.W., and Adams, E.N. "Pilot Study of a CAI Laboratory in German." Yorktown Heights, New York: IBM Corporation, Report RC-1974, December 1967, 25 pp.

Mosher, Ralph S. "Industrial Manipulators." Scientific American, vol. 211, no. 4, October 1964, pp. 88-96.

Moursund, D.G. How Computers Do It. Belmont, California: Wadsworth Publishing Company, 1969.

Mowshowitz, Abbe. The Conquest of Will: Information Processing in Human Affairs. Reading, Massachusetts: Addison-Wesley Publishing Company, 1976.

_____. "Information, Power, and Complexity." Part 1. Computers and People, vol. 25, no. 1, January 1976, pp. 23-27.

_____. "Information, Power, and Complexity - Part 2." Computers and People, vol. 25, no. 2, February 1976, pp. 20-22, 25-26.

_____. "Computing Power and Political Opportunism." Ithaca, New York: Cornell University, Department of Computer Science, Technical Report 76-274, March 1976, 24 pp.

_____. Inside Information: Computers in Fiction. Reading, Massachusetts: Addison-Wesley Publishing Company, 1977.

_____. "Computers and the Mechanization of Judgment." Vancouver, British Columbia: University of British Columbia, Department of Computer Science, Technical Report 77-3, April 1977, 33 pp.

Much, Marilyn. "Will Computers Outnumber Their Masters?" Industry Week, vol. 197, no. 6, 12 June 1978, pp. 66-78.

Muller, Don. "Personal Computers in Home and Business Applications." Computers and People, vol. 26, no. 12, December 1977, pp. 11-12, 20, 27.

Muller, Herbert J. The Children of Frankenstein. Bloomington, Indiana: Indiana University Press, 1971.

_____. "Education for the Future." American Scholar, vol. 41, no. 3, Summer 1972, pp. 377-388.

Mumford, Enid. "Implementing EDP Systems - A Sociological Perspective." Computer Bulletin, vol. 13, January 1969, pp. 10-13.

Mumford, Enid, and Sackman, Harold. "International Human Choice and Computers: Conference Retrospect and Propect." Santa Monica, California: The RAND Corporation, Report P-5258, June 1974, 33 pp.

_____., eds. Human Choice and Computers: Proceedings. New York, New York: North Holland Publishing Company, 1975.

Mumford, Lewis. Technics and Civilization. New York, New York: Harcourt Brace Jovanovich, 1963.

_____. The Myth of the Machine: Technics and Human Development. London, England: Secker and Warburg, 1967.

_____. The Myth of the Machine: The Pentagon of Power. New York, New York: Harcourt Brace Jovanovich, 1970.

Munson, George E. "Robots Quietly Take Their Places Alongside Humans on the Production Line to Raise Productivity - and do the 'Dirty Work.'" IEEE Spectrum, vol. 15, no. 10, October 1978, pp. 66-70.

Murdick, Robert G., and Ross, Joel E. "Future Management Information Systems - Part 1." Journal of Systems Management, vol. 23, no. 4, April 1972, pp. 22-25.

_____. "Future Management Information Systems - Part 2." Journal of Systems Management, vol. 23, no. 5, May 1972, pp. 32-35.

Musgrave, William. "The Computerized Work Station." Dun's Review, vol. 112, no. 1, July 1978, pp. 109, 111.

Myers, Charles A. The Impact of Computers on Management. Cambridge, Massachusetts: MIT Press, 1967.

_____. Computers in Knowledge-Based Fields. Cambridge, Massachusetts: MIT Press, 1970, 136 pp.

Myers, Edith. "Computer Security: Each Case is Different." Datamation, vol. 21, no. 4, April 1975, pp. 107-109.

_____. "Security: The Only Means to Privacy." Datamation, vol. 23, no. 5, May 1977, pp. 240-242.

Nadel, Laurie, and Wiener, Hesh. "Would You Sell a Computer to Hitler?" Computer Decisions, vol. 9, no. 2, February 1977, pp. 22-26.

Nance, Richard E., and Baker, Norman R. "Library Policy Structure: An Industrial Dynamics Study." Simulation, vol. 17, no. 3, September 1971, pp. 109-124.

Nanus, Burt; Wooten, Leland; and Borko, Harold. The Social Implications of the Use of Computers Across National Boundaries. Montvale, New Jersey: AFIPS Press, 1973.

Nanus, Burt, and Wooton, Michael L. "Implications of Multinational Computers." Business Horizons, February 1974, pp. 5-17.

Nathanson, R. "The Police Information Network of New York State." Computers and People, vol. 27, no. 3, March 1978, pp. 14-17.

Negley, Glenn. "Philosophical Views on the Value of Privacy." Law and Contemporary Problems, Spring 1966, pp. 319-325.

Negroponte, Nicholas. The Architecture Machine: Toward a More Human Environment. Cambridge, Massachusetts: MIT Press, 1970, 153 pp.

Neier, Aryeh. Dossier: The Secret Files They Keep on You. New York, New York: Stein and Day, 1975.

_____. "Privacy in a Free Society." Current, April 1975, pp. 45-53. From Dossier: The Secret Files They Keep on You.

Neill, Michael. "Some Thoughts on Reasons, Definitions and Tasks to Achieve 'Functional' Computer Literacy." SIGCSE Bulletin, vol. 9, no. 1, February 1977, pp. 175-177.

Nelson, Richard R.; Peck, Merlon J.; and Kalachek, Edward D. Technology, Economic Growth and Public Policy. Washington, D.C.: The Brookings Institution, 1967.

Nelson, Ronald H. "Computer Programming for Facilities Treating Developmentally Disabled Children." Computers and Society, vol. 8, no. 2, Summer 1977, pp. 14-17.

Nelson, Theodor H. Computer Lib/Dream Machines. Chicago, Illinois: Hugo's Book Service, 1974.

_____. "Computer Lib." Computer Decisions, vol. 6, no. 12, December 1974, pp. 48-50.

_____. The Home Computer Revolution. South Bend, Indiana: Ted Nelson, Publisher, 1978.

Neuman, Paul. "'Personal' Computers Undercut the Control of DP Departments." Administrative Management, vol. 39, no. 5, May 1978, pp. 71-75.

"New Horizons for Computers." Special report in Dun's Review, vol. 112, no. 1, July 1978.

Newborn, M. Computer Chess. New York, New York: Academic Press, 1975.

Newell, Allen, and others. Speech Understanding Systems. New York, New York: Elsevier-North Holland, 1973.

Newton, John M., and Van Dyke, Bill F. "Computer-Assisted Instruction: Performance and Attitudes." Journal of Educational Research, vol. 65, no. 7, March 1972, pp. 291-293.

Niblett, G.B.F. "Digital Information and the Privacy Problem." Paris, France: OECD Publications, 1971, 58 pp.

Nieburg, H.L. "In the Name of Science." Chicago, Illinois: Quadrangle Books, 1966.

Nielsen, Norman R., and others. "Effective Safeguards for Computer System Integrity." AFIPS Conference Proceedings, vol. 45, 7-10 June 1976, pp. 75-84.

Nievergelt, J., and Farrar, J.C. "What Machines Can and Cannot Do." Computing Surveys, vol. 4, no. 2, June 1972, pp. 81-96.

Nikolaieff, George A., ed. Computers and Society. New York, New York: H.W. Wilson Company, 1970, 226 pp.

Nilles, Jack M. "The Millennium or Armageddon?" <u>Data Management</u>, vol. 16, no. 12, December 1978, pp. 42-44. Personal computers.

Nishihara, H. Keith. "Visual Information Processing: Artificial Intelligence and the Sensorium of Sight." <u>Technology Review</u>, vol. 81, no. 1, October 1978, pp. 28-49.

Nixon, E.R. "The Computer's Role in a Changing World." <u>Data Systems</u>, March 1969, pp. 44-45.

Nolan, Richard L. "Computer Data Banks: The Future Is Now." <u>Harvard Business Review</u>, vol. 51, no. 5, September-October 1973, pp. 98-114.

Nolan, Richard L., and Knutsen, K. Eric. "The Computerization of the ABC Widget Company." <u>Datamation</u>, vol. 20, no. 4, April 1974, pp. 71-76.

Noll, A. Michael. "The Interactions of Computers and Privacy." <u>Honeywell Computer Journal</u>, vol. 7, no. 3, 1973, pp. 163-172.

Nordhaus, W.D. "World Dynamics: Measurement Without Data." <u>The Economic Journal</u>, December 1973, pp. 1156-1183. Critique of Jay Forrester's book <u>World Dynamics</u>.

Norman, Adrian. "Computer Frauds: Are They a Manageable Risk?" <u>Accountancy</u>, vol. 87, no. 998, October 1976, pp. 78-81.

Norrgard, David L. <u>Regional Law Enforcement</u>. Chicago, Illinois: Public Administration Service, 1969.

Norris, William C. "Technological Cooperation for World Survival." <u>Computers and People</u>, vol. 26 no. 5, May 1977, pp. 9-12, 24.

Norton, J.H. "Information Systems: Some Basic Considerations." <u>Management Review</u>, September 1969, pp. 2-8.

Nozick, Robert. <u>Anarchy, State and Utopia</u>. New York, New York: Basic Books, 1974.

Nugent, F.A. "Confidentiality in College Counseling Centers." <u>Personnel and Guidance Journal</u>, May 1969, pp. 872-877.

Nycum, Susan. "Legal Aspects of Computer Abuse." In <u>Computers - The Next 5 Years: Digest of Papers</u>, pp. 181-183. New York, New York: The Institute of Electrical and Electronics Engineers, Inc., Spring COMPCON76, IEEE Catalog No. 76CH1069-4(CR), February 1976.

O'Brien, James A. "The Cashless, Checkless Society." <u>Journal of Data Management</u>, vol. 6, no. 5, May 1968, pp. 28-32.

_____. "The Computer and Banking's Protection." <u>Banking</u>, September 1968, pp. 115-118.

_____. "How the Computer Revolutionizes Personnel Requirements." *Personnel Administration*, vol. 31, September 1968, pp. 28-32.

O'Brien, Terry, and Dugdale, Valerie. "Questionnaire Administration by Computer." *Journal of the Market Research Society*, vol. 20, no. 4, October 1978, pp. 228-237.

Odeh, Anna, and Cook, Louella. "Computer-Assisted Instruction: Example of a Complete Guide to Users." Yorktown Heights, New York: IBM Corporation, Report RC-2339, 16 January 1969, 186 pp.

Oden, Teresa, and Thompson, Christine, eds. *Computers and Public Policy*. Hanover, New Hampshire: Kiewit Computation Center, 1977.

OECD. *Gaps in Technology: Electronic Computers*. Paris, France: 1969.

_____. *Computer Utilization in Member Countries*. Paris, France: 1970.

_____. *Information for a Changing Society*. Paris, France: 1971.

_____. *Science, Growth, and Society*. Paris, France: 1971.

_____. *The Evaluation of the Performance of Computer Systems*. Paris, France: 1974.

Oettinger, Anthony G. "The Uses of Computers in Science." *Scientific American*, September 1966, pp. 161-166, 168-170, 172.

Oettinger, Anthony G., and Marks, Sema. *Run Computer Run: The Mythology of Educational Innovation*. Cambridge, Massachussets: Harvard University Press, 1969, 302 pp.

Olling, Gustav. "Experts Look Ahead to the Day of the Full-Blown Computer-Integrated Automatic Factory." *IEEE Spectrum*, vol. 15, no. 10, October 1978, pp. 66-66.

O'Neal, Fred. "The Role of Public Schools in Computer-Assisted Instruction: Individualized Instruction in a Kansas City Junior High School." *Educational Technology*, vol. 10, no. 3, March 1970, pp. 5-10.

Orchanian, Paul L. "Data Processing Techniques for Computers and Local Law Enforcement." *Law and Computer Technology*, vol. 2, May 1969, pp. 11-15.

Orr, Kenneth T. "Data Security and Privacy: Phase Two." *Infosystems*, vol. 23, no. 2, February 1976, pp. 34-35.

Orr, William D. *Conversational Computers*. New York, New York: John Wiley and Sons, 1968.

Orther, Everett H. "Computer Printed Enlargement." *Popular Science*, vol. 210, June 1977, pp. 92-93.

Orwell, George. _1984_. New York, New York: Harcourt Brace Jovanovich, 1949. Science fiction.

O'Toole, George. "Harmonica Bugs, Cloaks, and Silver Boxes." _Harper's_, June 1975, pp. 36-39.

O'Toole, John F., Jr. _Applications of Computers and Information Processing Systems in Education_. Santa Monica, California: System Development Corporation, 12 March 1965.

O'Toole, T. "White Collar Automation." _The Reporter_, vol. 29, 5 December 1963, pp. 24-27.

Ovellette, R.P.; Greeley, R.S.; and Overby, J.W., II. _Computer Techniques in Environmental Science_. New York, New York: Petrocelli/Charter Publishers, 1975.

Overby, Charles M. "Work Organization in an Information Era." _Industrial Engineering_, vol. 7, no. 10, October 1975, pp. 30-32.

Overman, Michael. _Understanding the Computer_. New York, New York: International Publishing Service, 1975.

Packard, Vance. _The Naked Society_. New York, New York: David McKay Company, 1964.

_____. "The People Shapers." _Saturday Review_, 20 August 1977, pp. 33-48. Excerpt.

Packer, Rod E. "The Automated Processing of People." _Computers and Automation_, vol. 15, no. 4, April 1966, pp. 20-23, 58.

Papert, Seymour. _The Artificial Intelligence of Hubert L. Dreyfus: A Budget of Fallacies_. Cambridge, Massachusetts: MIT Press, 1968.

Papert, Seymour, and Solomon, Cynthia. "Twenty Things to Do with a Computer." _Educational Technology_, vol. 12, no. 4, April 1972, pp. 9-18. Teaching computer programming.

Parker, A.J., and Silbey, V. "User Meets Computer: A Problem of 'Upward Compatibility.'" _Computers and People_, vol. 27, no. 10, October 1978, pp. 15-17.

Parker, Donn B. "Computers and Public Concern." Palo Alto, California: Control Data Corporation, March 1968.

_____. "Rules of Ethics in Information Processing." _Communications of the ACM_, vol. 11, no. 3, March 1968, pp. 198, 200-201.

_____. "Professional Conduct in Information Processing." _Communications of the ACM_, vol. 11, no. 3, March 1968, pp. 199.

_____. _Computer-Related Crime and Data Security_. Menlo Park, California: Stanford Research Institute, 1972, 29 pp.

_____. "The Antisocial Use of Computers." Computers and Automation, vol. 21, no. 8, August 1972, pp. 22-36.

_____. "Computer Security: Some Easy Things to Do." Computer Decisions, vol. 6, no. 1, January 1974, pp. 17-18.

_____. Computer Abuse Assessment. Menlo Park, California: Stanford Research Institute, 1975.

_____. Crime by Computer: Starting New Kinds of Million-Dollar Fraud, Theft, Larceny, and Embezzlement. New York, New York: Charles Scribner and Sons, 1976, 308 pp.

_____. "Computer and Data Abuse." In Digest of Papers, pp. 184-186. New York, New York: The Institute of Electrical and Electronics Engineers, Inc., Spring COMPCON76, IEEE Catalog No. 76CH1069-4(CR), February 1976.

_____. "Computer Abuse Perpetrators and Vulnerabilities of Computer Systems." AFIPS Conference Proceedings, vol. 45, 7-10 June 1976, pp. 65-73.

Parker, Donn B., and Nycum, Susan. "The New Criminal." Datamation, January 1974, pp. 56-58.

Parker, Edwin B. "Democracy and Information Processing." Computers and Society, Winter 1974, pp. 3-6.

Parker, Edwin B., and Dunn, D.A. "Information Technology: Its Social Potential." Science, vol. 176, 1972, pp. 1392-1399.

Parker, Ralph H. "Not a Shared System: An Account of a Computer Operated Designed Specifically and Solely for Library Use at the University of Missouri." Library Journal, vol. 92, 1 November 1967, pp. 3967-3970.

Parker, Robert A. "The Aesthetic World of the Computer." Personal Computing, vol. 2, no. 1, January 1978, pp. 56-59. Collaboration of artist Manuel Felguerez with electrical engineer Mayer Sasson.

Parkhill, D.F. The Challenge of the Computer Utility. Reading, Massachusetts: Addison-Wesley Publishing Company, 1966.

Parkman, Ralph. The Cybernetic Society. Elmsford, New York: Pergamon Press, 1972.

Parkoff, Stephen B. "The Form and Function of a National Educational Data Center." Data Processing Magazine, February 1968, pp. 34-37.

Parsons, R.B. "Impact of the Computer on Management Principles." Advanced Management Journal, vol. 33, October 1968, pp. 51-53.

Parsons, William W. "The Implications of the Information Sciences for Intergovernmental Cooperation in Communications and Exchange of Information." Computers and Automation, vol. 18, no. 4, April 1969, pp. 34-37.

"Participation II - A Social Responsibilities Report." *Computers and People*, vol. 26, no. 10, October 1977, p. 16.

Patrick, D.K. "File-Organization Security in a Real-Time System." *IBM Technical Disclosure Bulletin*, vol. 13, no. 4, September 1970, pp. 1030-1031.

Patrick, Robert L. "Computing in the 1970's." *Datamation*, vol. 13, no. 1, January 1967, pp. 27-30.

Patrick, Robert L., and Dahl, Aubrey. "Voting Systems: Los Angeles Doesn't Have One." *Datamation*, vol. 16, no. 5, May 1970, pp. 81-82.

Patterson, C.H. "Pupil Personnel Services in the Automated School." *Personnel and Guidance Journal*, vol. 48, no. 2, 1969, pp. 101-110. Prediction.

Peckham, Herbert D. "Computers, Confusion and Complacency." *Computers and Education*, vol. 1, no. 1, 1976, pp. 39-45.

Peiper, J. *Leisure, the Basis of Culture*. New York, New York: Random House, 1963, 127 pp.

Pepinsky, Harold B. *People and Information*. Elmsford, New York: Pergamon Press, 1970.

Peralta, Luis A., and Skrabal, Robert J. "Space Planning with Computer Graphics." *Record*, vol. 56, no. 9, October 1978, pp. 241-245. Computerized "drafting, storing, and retrieval of office layouts."

Perry, James M. *The New Politics: The Expanding Technology of Political Manipulation*. New York, New York: Clarkson N. Potter, Inc., 1968.

Peter, L.J., and Hull, R. *The Peter Principle*. New York, New York: William Morrow and Company, Inc., 1969.

Peters, Bernard. "Security Considerations in Multi-Programmed Computer Systems." *AFIPS Conference Proceedings*, SJCC, vol. 30, 18-20 April 1967, pp. 283-286.

Petersen, H.E., and Turn, Rein. "System Implications of Information Privacy." Santa Monica, California: The RAND Corporation, Report P-3504, April 1967. Also in *AFIPS Conference Proceedings*, SJCC, vol. 30, 18-20 April 1967, pp. 291-300.

Petruschell, R.L. "Sixty Years of Growth in Computing and Data-Processing Capability." Santa Monica, California: The RAND Corporation, Report P-1932, 8 March 1960, 4 pp.

Phillipson, M. *Automation, Implications for the Future*. New York, New York: Random House, 1962.

Phister, Montgomery, Jr. "Analyzing Computer Technology Costs - Part 1: Development and Manufacturing." Computer Design, vol. 17, no. 9, September 1978, pp. 91-98.

_____. "Analyzing Computer Technology Costs - Part 2: Maintenance." Computer Design, vol. 17, no. 10, October 1978, pp. 109-118.

Piecewicz, Robert E. "Computers and Society: Some Principles, Theorems, and Assertions." Computers and People, vol. 26, no. 4, April 1977, pp. 13-16.

Pileggi, Nicholas. "Secrets of a Private Eye." New York, 4 October 1976, pp. 38-45.

Pirsig, Robert M. Zen and the Art of Motorcycle Maintenance. New York, New York: William Morrow and Company, Inc., 1974, 406 pp. Relationship between people and machines.

Plants, John R. "Michigan's Law Enforcement Information Network." Datamation, vol. 15, no. 6, June 1969, pp. 106-108.

Poage, James. "Federal Law Protecting Your Right to Privacy." Computers and Society, Summer 1975, pp. 3-8.

Pohland, Paul A., and Smith, Louis M. "Computer-Assisted Instruction: Issues for Decision Making." Administrator's Notebook, vol. 20, no. 1, pp. 1-4.

Polanyi, M. Personal Knowledge. New York, New York: Harper Torchbooks, 1964.

Pollack, Jack Harrison. "Six Ways Your Vote Can Be Stolen." Harper's, November 1972, pp. 88-89.

Pool, Ithiel de Sola, and others. Candidates, Issues, and Strategies. Cambridge, Massachusetts: MIT Press, 1964.

Popek, G.J. "On the Technical State of the Art in Computer Security." In How to Make Computers Easier to Use: Digest of Papers, pp. 40-41. New York, New York: The Institute of Electrical and Electronics Engineers, Inc., Fall COMPCON75, IEEE Catalog No. 75CH0988-6C, 9-11 September 1975.

Poppel, Harvey L. "The Information Revolution: Winners and Losers." Harvard Business Review, vol. 56, no. 1, January-February 1978, pp. 14, 16, 159.

Porter, W. Thomas. EDP Controls and Auditing. Belmont, California: Wadsworth Publishing Company, 1974.

Porter, William E. "The Privacy Act of 1974: A Look at it From a Combined Technical and Legal Perspective." Computers and People, vol. 25, no. 12, December 1976, pp. 10-13.

Postley, J.A. Computers and People. New York, New York: McGraw-Hill Book Company, 1960.

Powers, Richard F., and Dickson, Gary W. "MisProject Management: Myths, Opinions, and Reality." *California Management Review*, vol. 15, no. 3, Spring 1973, pp. 147-156.

Powers, Thomas. "The Government Is Watching." *Atlantic*, October 1972, pp. 51-63.

Press, Lawrence I. "Arguments for a Moratorium on the Construction of a Community Information Utility." *Communications of the ACM*, vol. 17, no. 12, December 1974, pp. 674-678.

Pressey, Sidney L. "Basic Unresolved Teaching-Machine Problems." *Theory into Practice*, vol. 1, February 1962, pp. 30-37.

_____. "Teaching Machine (and Learning Theory) Crisis." *Journal of Applied Psychology*, vol. 47, no. 1, February 1963, pp. 1-6.

Pressman, I. "Computer-Assisted Instruction: A Survey." *IEEE Transactions on Education*, vol. 13, September 1970, pp. 134-141.

Price, Dennis G. "Automation in State and Local Governments." *Datamation*, vol. 13, no. 3, March 1967, pp. 22-25.

Price, Dennis G., and Mulvihill, Dennis E. "The Present and Future Use of Computers in State Government." *Public Administration Review*, vol. 25, June 1965, pp. 142-150.

Prisendorf, Anthony. "The Computer vs. the Bill of Rights." *The Nation*, 31 October 1966, pp. 449-452.

"Privacy and the Computer: A Conversation with Bob Henderson." *Data Systems News*, August-September 1970, pp. 16-17.

Privacy and the National Data Bank Concept: Thirty-Fifth Report. United States House of Representatives, Committee on Government Operations, 90th Congress, 2nd Session, 2 August 1968, 34 pp.

Privacy and the Rights of Federal Employees. United States Senate, Committee on the Judiciary, Subcommittee on Constitutional Rights, 89th Congress, 2nd Session, September-October 1966. Hearings.

Privacy in the Mail. United States House of Representives, Subcommittee on Postal Operations, Committee on Post Office and Civil Service, 90th Congress, 2nd Session, 23-24 July 1968. Hearings.

"Privacy Protection Study Commission Issues Final Report." *Software Digest*, vol. 9, no. 28, 14 July 1977, pp. 1, 6-9.

Protecting Privacy and the Rights of Federal Employees. United States Senate, Committee on the Judiciary, 90th Congress, 1st Session, 21 August 1967. Report.

"Protection of Electronic Computer/Data Processing Equipment." Boston, Massachusetts: National Fire Protection Association, Pamphlet No. 75, 1968.

Provencher, Lauri. "Two Constitutional Rights Equal One Political Dilemma." *The Center Magazine*, vol. 9, no. 1, January-February 1976, pp. 7-14. Conflict between the right to privacy and the right to know.

Pryor, T. Allen, and others. "HELP - A Computer System for Medical Decision Making." *Computer*, January 1975, pp. 34-38.

Psychological Tests and Constitutional Rights. United States Senate, Committee on the Judiciary, Subcommittee on Constitutional Rights, 89th Congress, 1st Session, 7-10 June 1965. Hearings.

"Public Access to Government-Held Computerized Information." *Northwestern University Law Review*, vol. 68, no. 2, May-June 1973, pp. 433-462. Comment.

Puccetti, Roland. "God and the Robots: A Philosophical Fable." *The Personalist*, vol. 56, no. 1, Winter 1975, pp. 29-30. Fiction.

Putnam, Arnold. "The Human Side of Management Systems." *Business Automation*, vol. 15, no. 11, November 1968, pp. 42-48.

Puz, Richard. "A Computer that People Can Talk To." *Computers and People*, vol. 26, no. 5, May 1977, pp. 2-3.

Pylyshyn, Zenon W., ed. *Perspectives on the Computer Revolution*. Englewood Cliffs, New Jersey: Prentice-Hall, Inc., 1970, 576 pp.

_____. "How Can Machines Do What Their Makers Can't?" *Computers and Automation*, vol. 19, no. 5, May 1970, pp. 22-25.

Quillan, M. Ross. "The Teachable Language Comprehender: A Simulation Program and Theory of Language." *Communications of the ACM*, vol. 12, no. 8, August 1969, pp. 459-476.

Quinn, E.M. "One Way to Get More Economical CAI Materials." Yorktown Heights, New York: IBM Corporation, Report NC-535, 23 September 1965, 4 pp.

_____. "A CAI Reading Program: Preliminary Field Test." Yorktown Heights, New York: IBM Corporation, Report NC-576, January 1966, 5 pp.

_____. "Computer-Assisted Instruction Arithmetic Drill and Practice Exercises." Yorktown Heights, New York: IBM Corporation, Report RC-1929, October 1967, 8 pp.

Quinn, E.M., and Odeh, A. "Computer-Assisted Instruction Arithmetic Drill and Practice Exercises: Description of Organization and Logic." Yorktown Heights, New York: IBM Corporation, Report RC-1898, September 1967, 8 pp.

Quinney, Richard. *The Social Reality of Crime*. Boston, Massachusetts: Little, Brown and Company, 1962.

Quinton, A.M. <u>Utilitarian Ethics</u>. New York, New York: St. Martin's Press, 1973.

Raben, Joseph. "Computer and Literacy Studies." <u>Quarterly Bulletin</u>, vol. 7, no. 4, Summer 1967, pp. 16-19.

_____. "Computer and the Values of Literature." <u>Educational Record</u>, Fall 1969, pp. 432-441.

Rachels, James. "Why Privacy Is Important." <u>Philosophy and Public Affairs</u>, Summer 1975, pp. 323-333.

Raiffa, H. <u>Design Analysis: Introductory Lectures on Choices under Uncertainty</u>. Reading, Massachusetts: Addison-Wesley Publishing Company, 1968.

Ramo, Simon. "A New Technique of Education." <u>Engineering and Science Monthly</u>, vol. 21, October 1957, pp. 17-22.

_____. "The Computer and Our Changing Society." <u>AFIPS Conference Proceedings</u>, FJCC, vol. 27, Part 2, November-December 1965, pp. 5-10.

_____. <u>Cure for Chaos</u>. New York, New York: David McKay, 1968.

Randell, B., ed. <u>The Orgins of Digital Computers</u>. New York, New York: Springer-Verlag, 1973.

Raphael, Bertram. <u>The Thinking Computer: Mind Inside Matter</u>. San Francisco, California: W.H. Freeman and Company, 1976.

Raskin, A.H. "Automation: Road to Lifetime Jobs?" <u>Saturday Review</u>, vol. 47, 28 November 1964, pp. 1-16.

Rathe, Gaustave H., Jr. "Computer-Assisted Instruction, Promising New Tools for Teaching Deaf Students." <u>The Volta Review</u>, vol. 70, no. 6, September 1968, pp. 447-452.

Redford, K.J. <u>Information Systems in Management</u>. Reston, California: Reston Publishing Company, 1973.

Reich, Charles A. <u>The Greening of America: How the Youth Revolution Is Trying to Make America Liveable</u>. New York, New York: Random House, 1970.

Reichardt, Jasia. <u>Cybernetic Serendipity</u>. New York, New York: Frederick A. Praeger, 1969.

_____. <u>Cybernetics, Art, and Ideas</u>. New York, New York: New York Graphic Society, 1971.

_____. <u>The Computer in Art</u>. New York, New York: Van Nostrand Reinhold Company, 1971.

_____. Robots: Fact, Fiction, and Prediction. New York, New York: Penguin Book, Inc., 1978.

Reiman, Jeffrey H. "Privacy, Intimacy, and Personhood." Philosophy and Public Affairs, vol. 6, no. 1, Fall 1976, pp. 26-44. Critique of Charles Fried's An Anatomy of Values: Problems of Personal and Social Choice.

Reinstedt, Robert N., and Berger, Raymond M. "Certification: A Suggested Approach to Acceptance." Datamation, vol. 19, no. 11, November 1973, pp. 97-100.

Reistad, Dale L. "Credit Cards: Stepping Stones to the Checkless Society?" Computers and Automation, vol. 16, no. 1, January 1967, pp. 26-27, 46.

Remy, Raymond. "Survey Discloses Tremendous Growth of Data Processing in California Cities." Western City, July 1969, pp. 13-14, 31.

Rendleman, Jackson E. "The Other Side of Privacy." Armed Forces Comptroller, August 1977, pp. 8-9, 29.

Resnick, Lauren B. "Programmed Instruction and the Teaching of Complex Intellectual Skills: Problems and Prospects." Harvard Educational Review, vol. 33, 1963, pp. 439-471.

Rezler, Julius. Automation and Industrial Labor. New York, New York: Random House, 1969.

_____. "Automation and the Personnel Manager." Advanced Management Journal, vol. 32, January 1969, pp. 76-81.

Reznikoff, N., and others. "Attitudes Toward Computers Among Employees of a Psychiatric Hospital." Mental Hygiene, vol. 51, July 1967, pp. 419-425.

Rhee, H.A. Office Automation in Social Perspective - The Progress and Social Implications of EDP. Oxford, England: Basil Blackwell, 1968.

Rice, Jean M. My Friend the Computer. Minneapolis, Minnesota: T.S. Denison and Company, Inc., 1976.

Richardson, Robert A. "Some Social Consequences of Technological Success." Hastings Center Report, November 1974, pp. 4-6.

Rickert, Jerome P. "On-Line Support for Manufacturing." Datamation, vol. 21, no. 7, July 1975, pp. 46-48.

Rickover, Hyman G. "Humanistic Technology." American Behavioral Scientist, vol. 9, January 1965, pp. 3-8.

Riley, Wallace B. "Computer Networks Are Taking on the Heavyweight Computations." Electronics, 2 May 1974, pp. 98-107.

Roberts, Jerome J. "Computer-Generated Evidence." *Data Management*, November 1974, pp. 20-21.

Robertson, Edward L. "Computers in Developing Nations." *Computers and Society*, Summer 1976, pp. 7-9.

Robinson, Guy. "How to Tell Your Friends from Machines." *Mind*, vol. 81, no. 324, October 1972, pp. 504-518.

Robinson, Stanley. "The National Crime Information Center (NCIC) of the FBI: Do We Want It?" *Computers and Automation*, vol. 20, no. 6, June 1971, pp. 16-19.

Rockart, John F. "Associative Learning Projects in Computer-Assisted Instruction." *Educational Technology*, vol. 11, no. 11, November 1971, pp. 17-23.

Rockefeller, Nelson A. *The Future of Federalism*. Cambridge, Massachusetts: Harvard University Press, 1964.

Rodgers, William. *Think: A Biography of the Watsons and IBM*. New York, New York: Stein and Day, 1969.

_____. "The Bride Came COD: Corruption in the Computer Industry." *Computer Decisions*, vol. 8, no. 9, September 1976, pp. 66, 72, 74-75.

Rodman, John A. "Computerized Faculty Information System." *Journal of the Society of Research Administration*, vol. 9, no. 2, Fall 1977, pp. 9-14.

Rogers, James L. "Current Problems in CAI." *Datamation*, vol. 14, no. 9, September 1968, pp. 28-33.

Rokeach, M. *The Nature of Human Values*. New York, New York: The Free Press, 1973.

Ronayne, Maurice F. "The Personnel Side of Automated Data Processing." *Public Personnel Review*, vol. 21, no. 4, October 1960, pp. 243-248.

Rose, Sanford. "More Bang for the Buck: The Magic of Electronic Banking." *Fortune*, vol. 95, no. 5, May 1977, pp. 202-205, 208, 212, 216, 218, 221, 223, 226.

_____. "Checkless Banking is Bound to Come." *Fortune*, June 1977, pp. 118-121, 124, 126, 128, 130.

Rosen, Saul. "Electronic Computers: A Historical Survey." *Computing Surveys*, vol. 1, no. 1, March 1969, pp. 7-36.

Rosenbaum, P.S. "The Computer as a Learning Environment for Foreign Language Instruction." Yorktown Heights, New York: IBM Corporation, Report RC-2352, December 1968, 12 pp.

Rosenbausm, Robert. "Toward the Automated Workbook: A New Direction for CAI." Educational Technology, vol. 12, no. 5, May 1972, pp. 36-38.

Rosenberg, Jerry M. The Computer Prophets. New York, New York: Collier-Macmillan, 1969.

_____. "Human and Organizational Implications of Computer Privacy." AFIPS Conference Proceedings, vol. 45, 7-10 June 1976, pp. 39-43.

Rosenberg, M., and others. "Attitudes of Nursing Students Toward Computers." Nursing Outlook, vol. 15, July 1967, pp. 44-46.

_____., and others. "How Patients Feel About Computers." Hospital and Community Psychiatry, November 1967, pp. 36-38.

Rosenblatt, Alfred I. "Industrial Automatic Control Proliferates." Electronics, 11 July 1974, pp. 83-87.

Rosenblith, Walter A. "On Cybernetics and the Human Brain." American Scholar, vol. 35, no. 2, Spring 1966, pp. 243-248.

Rosenfeld, Arnold. "A Complete Electronic Newspaper?" The Antioch Review, Spring-Summer 1977, pp. 171-179.

Rosove, Perry E. Developing Computer-Based Information Systems. New York, New York: John Wiley and Sons, Inc., 1968.

Ross, Ian M., an interview with. "Technology Today and Tommorrow." Record, vol. 56, no. 8, September 1978, pp. 194-201.

Ross, Irwin. "Soviet DP Industry Still Lagging After 25 Years." Computerworld, vol. 12, no. 50, 11 December 1978, p. 97.

Rossman, Michael. "Implications of Computer Memory." Computers and Society, Winter 1975, pp. 7-10.

Rossum, Robert. "Robots as Household Pets." Interface Age, April 1977, pp. 32-34, 36-37.

Roszak, Theodore. The Making of a Counterculture: Reflections on the Technocratic Society and Its Youthful Opposition. New York, New York: Doubleday and Company, 1969.

_____. Where the Wasteland Ends. New York, New York: Doubleday and Company, 1972.

Rothery, Brian. The Myth of the Computer. Brooklyn Heights, New York: Beekman Publishing, Inc., 1971.

Rothman, Stanley, and Mosmann, Charles. Computers and Society - The Technology and Its Social Implications. 2nd edition. Palo Alto, California: Science Research Associates, Inc., 1976, 423 pp.

Rowan, Charles R. "Information Systems Technology in State Government." State Government, vol. 44, no. 2, Spring 1971, pp. 113-120.

Rowan, Ford. _Technospies_. New York, New York: G.P. Putnam's Sons, 1978.

Rowat, Donald C., ed. _The Ombudsman - Citizen's Defender_. London, England: Allen and Unwin, Ltd., 1965.

Rowe, B.C. _Privacy, Computers, and You_. Manchester, England: NCC Publications, 1972.

Rubin, Sylvan. "A Simple Instructional Language." _Computer Decisions_, vol. 5, no. 10, October 1973, pp. 17-18.

Ruebhausen, Oscar M., and Brim, Orville, G., Jr. "Privacy and Behavioral Research." _Columbia Law Review_, vol. 65, November 1965, pp. 1184-1211.

Ruggles, Richard. "How a Data Bank Might Operate." _Think_, May-June 1969, pp. 22-23.

Rusch, R.B. _Man's Marvelous Computer: The Next Quarter Century_. New York, New York: Simon and Schuster, 1970.

Russo, Paul M., and others. "Microprocessors in Consumer Products." _Proceedings of the IEEE_, vol. 66, no. 2, February 1978, pp. 131-141.

Ryan, Frank B. "The Electronic Voting System for the United States House of Representatives." _Computer_, vol. 5, no. 6, November-December 1972, pp. 32-37.

Rychel, Dwight F. "Computer Applications in Petroleum Reservoir Research." _Computers and Industrial Engineering_, vol. 1, no. 2, 1977, pp. 139-144.

Sable, Robert W. "Law Enforcement Data Processing." _Communications of the ACM_, vol. 8, April 1965, p. 248.

Sackman, Harold. _Computers, System Science, and Evolving Society_. New York, New York: John Wiley and Sons, 1967.

_____. _Mass Information Utilities and Social Excellence_. New York, New York: Auerbach Publishers Inc., 1971.

Sackman, Harold, and Boehm, B. _Planning Community Information Utilities_. Montvale, New Jersey: AFIPS Press, 1972.

Sackman, Harold, and Borko, H., eds. _Computers and the Problems of Society_. Montvale, New Jersey: AFIPS Press, 1972.

Sackman, Harold, and Nie, Norman, eds. _The Information Utility and Social Choice_. Montvale, New Jersey: AFIPS Press, 1970, 299 pp.

Sadler, P. "Automation: Some Sociological Considerations." _Computer Bulletin_, vol. 13, July 1969, pp. 214-219.

Safeguarding Taxpayer Information - An Evaluation of the Proposed Computerized Tax Administration System. United States Department of the Treasury, Internal Revenue Service, Report LCD-76-115, 17 January 1977.

Sagan, Carl. "In Praise of Robots." Computers and People, vol. 24, no. 5, May 1975, pp. 8-12.

_____. The Dragons of Eden. New York, New York: Random House, 1977.

Sage, David M. "Information Systems: A Brief Look into History." Datamation, November 1968, pp. 63-69.

Salasin, John. "A Control Systems Model of Privacy." AFIPS Conference Proceedings, vol. 45, 7-10 June 1976, pp. 45-51.

Salisbury, Alan B. "Computers and Education: Toward Agreement on Terminology." Educational Technology, vol. 11, no. 9, September 1971, pp. 35-40.

Saltzer, J.H., and Schroeder, M.D. "The Protection of Information in Computer Systems." Proceedings of the IEEE, vol. 63, no. 9, September 1975, pp. 1278-1308.

Sammet, Jean E. "Description of a Course Given on 'Computers in the Humanities and Social Science.'" Gaithersburg, Maryland: IBM Corporation, Form FSD-74-0301, February 1975, 12 pp.

Samuel, Arthur L. "Some Studies in Machine Learning, Using the Game of Checkers." IBM Journal of Research and Development, vol. 3, July 1959, pp. 210-229.

_____. "Some Moral and Technical Consequences of Automation - A Refutation." Science, 16 September 1960, pp. 741-742. Refutation of Norbert Wiener's article in Science of 6 May 1960.

Sanders, Donald H. Computers and Management in a Changing Society. New York, New York: McGraw-Hill Book Company, 1970.

_____. Computers in Society. 2nd edition. New York, New York: McGraw-Hill Book Company, 1977, 458 pp.

Sanders, N. The Corporate Computer: How to Live with an Ecological Intrusion. New York, New York: McGraw-Hill Book Company, 1973.

Sapolsky, Harvey M. "Technological Change and Politics." Datamation, vol. 13, no. 10, October 1967, pp. 47, 49-50, 53-54.

Sawyer, Jack, and Schechter, Howard. "Computers, Privacy, and the National Data Center: The Responsibility of Social Scientists." American Psychologist, vol. 23, no. 11, November 1968, pp. 810-818.

Scaletta, Phillip J., Jr. "The Computer as a Threat to Individual Privacy." Data Management, vol. 9, no. 1, January 1971, pp. 18-23.

Scanlon, Thomas. "Thomson on Privacy." Philosophy and Public Affairs, Summer 1975, pp. 315-322.

_____. "Nozick on Rights, Liberty, and Property." Philosophy and Public Affairs, vol. 6, no. 1, Fall 1976, pp. 3-25. Comment on Anarchy, State and Utopia by R. Nozick.

Schank, R.C., and Colby, K.M. Computer Models of Thought and Language. San Francisco, California: W.H. Freeman and Company, 1973.

Schild, W.; Lunenfeld, B.; and Gavish, B. "Computer-Aided Diagnosis with an Application to Endocrinology." IBM Journal of Research and Development, September 1978, pp. 518-532.

Schiller, Herber I. Mass Communications and American Empire. New York, New York: M. Kelley Publisher, 1969.

Schlager, Kenneth J. "The Impact of Computers on Urban Transportation." AFIPS Conference Proceedings, FJCC, vol. 27, Part 2, November-December 1965, pp. 51-55.

Schneider, Ben Ross, Jr. Travels in Computerland: Or, Incompatibilities and Interfaces. Reading, Massachusetts: Addison-Wesley Publishing Company, 1974.

Schoen, Harold L. "CAI Development and Good Educational Practice." Educational Technology, vol. 14, no. 4, April 1974, pp. 54-56.

Schoolman, H.M., and Bernstein, L.M. "Computer Use in Diagnosis, Prognosis, and Therapy." Science, vol. 200, no. 4344, 26 May 1978, pp. 925-931.

Schroer, Bernard J. "The Doctor (and Computer) Will See You Now." Journal of Systems Management, vol. 24, no. 3, March 1973, pp. 33-37.

Schultz, Brad. "DP Crime Data Center to Assist Prosecutors." Computerworld, vol. 12, no. 34, 21 August 1978, pp. 1, 4.

Schumacher, B.G. Computer Dynamics in Public Administration. Washington, D.C.: Spartan, 1967

Schurdak, J.J. "An Approach to the Use of Computers in the Instructional Processes and an Evaluation." Yorktown Heights, New York: IBM Corporation, Report RC-1432, July 1965, 38 pp.

Schwartz, B. "The Social Psychology of Privacy." American Journal of Sociology, vol. 73, May 1968, pp. 741-752.

Schwartz, E.S. Overkill: The Decline of Technology in Modern Civilization. New York, New York: Ballantine Books, 1971.

Schwartz, H.A., and Long, H.S. "Initial Attitudes of Prospective Students Toward Computer-Assisted Instruction." Poughkeepsie, New York: IBM Corporation, Technical Report 00.1273, May 1965, 11 pp.

_____. "Instruction by Computer: Motives and Methods." Poughkeepsie, New York: IBM Corporation, Technical Report 00.1404, February 1966, 19 pp.

_____. "A Study of Remote Industrial Training via Computer-Assisted Instruction." Poughkeepsie, New York: IBM Corporation, Technical Report 00.1417, March 1966, 19 pp.

_____. "A Study of Computer-Assisted Instruction in Industrial Training." Poughkeepsie, New York: IBM Corporation, Technical Report 00.1419, March 1966, 7 pp.

Schweinfurth, D.E. "The Coming Computer Utility - Laissez-Faire Licensing or Regulation." Computer Digest, vol. 3, May 1968, pp. 11-14.

Sclossberg, Edwin, and others. The Home Computer Handbook. New York, New York: Sterling Publishing Company, Inc., 1978.

Scoma, Louis, Jr. "The EDP Auditor." Data Management, May 1977, pp. 15-17.

Sedelow, Sally Yeates. "Language Analysis in the Humanities." Communications of the ACM, July 1972, pp. 644-647.

Seliger, Susan. "Check Privacy...Your Banker May Not Try to Keep Out Snoops in Wake of Judgment." The National Observer, 15 May 1976, p. 8.

Seligman, B.B. Most Notorious Victory, Man in an Age of Automation. New York, New York: The Free Press, 1966.

Seltzer, Robert A. "Computer-Assisted Instruction: What it Can and Cannot Do." American Psychologist, vol. 26, no. 4, April, pp. 373-377.

Semling, Harold V., Jr. "Congress and the Computer." Law and Computer Technology, vol. 2, no. 11, November 1969, pp. 7-13.

_____. "Future of East-West EDP Trade." Law and Computer Technology, vol. 2, no. 12, December 1969, pp. 16-25.

Sesser, S.N. "Big Brother Keeps Tabs on Insurance Buyers." The New Republic, April 1968, pp. 11-12.

Shankar, K.S. "The Total Computer Security Problem: An Overview." Computer, vol. 10, no. 6, June 1977, pp. 50-62, 71-73.

Shannon, Claude E. "Communication Theory of Secrecy Systems." Bell System Technical Journal, vol. 28, no. 4, October 1949, pp. 656-715.

_____. "Computers and Automata." Proceedings of the IRE, October 1953, pp. 1234-1241.

Shapiro, Norman. "A Computer and Its Man." Santa Monica, California: The RAND Corportion, Report P-5681, June 1976, 5 pp.

Shapiro, Robert M., and Hardt, Pamela. "The Impact of Computer Technology - A Case Study: The Dairy Industry." Computers and People, March 1976, pp. 8-13.

Shapley, Deborah. "Central Crime Computer Project Draws Mixed Reviews." Science, vol. 197, no. 4299, 8 July 1977, pp. 138-141.

_____. "Crime Computer Abused." Science, 8 July 1977, p. 139.

Sharpe, W.F. The Economics of Computers. New York, New York: Columbia University Press, 1969.

Sheahan, D.T. "A Contribution to the Discussion of Ethics." Computer Bulletin, February 1970, pp. 43-44.

_____. "BCS - Alteration to Articles." Computer Bulletin, February 1970, pp. 45-47. Professional ethics and disciplinary procedure.

Sheldon, Eleanor Bernert, and Moore, Wilbert E., eds. Indicators of Social Change: Concepts and Measurements. New York, New York: Russell Sage Foundation, 1968.

Shenker, I. "Computers Hum As the Saints Go Marching In." New York Times, 5 February 1976, p. 33. "Computerized study of 1500 saints to analyze the role of religion in society."

Shepard, J.M. Automation and Alienation: A Study of Office and Factory Workers. Cambridge, Massachusetts: MIT Press, 1971, 163 pp.

Sheridan, Philip. "Protect Your Computer Installation from Foreign Threats." Management World, vol. 7, no. 10, October 1978, pp. 27-29.

Sheridan, Thomas B. "Progress Report of the MIT Community Dialog Project." In Proceedings of the 1973 International Conference on Cybernetics and Society, pp. 139-144. New York, New York: The Institute of Electrical and Electronics Engineers, Inc., November 1973.

Shorter, Edward. The Historian and the Computer. Englewood Cliffs, New Jersey: Prentice-Hall, Inc., 1971.

Shubik, Martin. "Bibliography on Simulation, Gaming, Artificial Intelligence and Allied Topics." Journal of the American Statistical Association, vol. 55, December 1960, pp. 736-751.

_____. "Information, Rationality, and Free Choice in a Future Democratic Society." Daedalus, vol. 96, Summer 1967, pp. 777-778.

Shultz, G.P., and Whisler, T.L., eds. Management Organization and the Computer. Glencoe, Illinois: The Free Press, 1960.

Siegel, A.J. The Impact of Computers on Collective Bargaining. Cambridge, Massachusetts: MIT Press, 1969.

Silberman, Charles E. "The Real News about Automation." Fortune, vol. 71, no. 1, January 1965, pp. 124-127, 220-222, 227.

_____. The Myths of Automation. New York, New York: Harper and Row, Publishers, 1966.

Silberman, Harry F. "Self-Teaching Devices and Programmed Materials." Review of Educational Research, vol. 32, no. 2, April 1962, pp. 179-193.

_____. "The Digital Computer in Education." Phi Delta Kappan, vol. 43, May 1962, pp. 345-350.

Silver, Gerald A., and Silver, Joan B. Data Processing in Business. New York, New York: Harcourt Brace Jovanovich, 1973.

Simmons, Webb. "Computer Modeling." Personal Computing, vol. 1, no. 5, September-October 1977, pp. 74-81. The problems and techniques of "putting the real world onto the computer."

Simon, Herbert A. The New Science of Management Decision. New York, New York: Harper and Row, Publishers, 1960. Computer effect on the management of business organizations.

_____. The Shape of Automation for Men and Management. New York, New York: Harper and Row, Publishers, 1965.

_____. "A Computer for Everyman." American Scholar, vol. 35, no. 2, Spring 1966, pp. 258-264.

_____. "Management by Machine." Management Review, vol. 49, November 1966, pp. 12-19, 68-80.

_____. "What Computers Mean for Man and Society." Science, vol. 195, no. 4283, 18 May 1977, pp. 1186-1191.

_____. "Computers: Changing Man's View of Himself." Current, no. 193, May-June 1977, pp. 39-51. From "What Computers Mean for Man and Society," Science, 18 May 1977.

Simon, William E. "The Great American Challenges: Education and Ethics." Financial Executive, vol. 45, no. 4, April 1977, pp. 34-39.

Simonsen, Roger H. "Coaching/Prompting: The Answer for CAI." Infosystems, vol. 24, no. 1, January 1977, pp. 64-66.

Simonsen, Roger H., and Renshaw, Kent S. "CAI - Boon or Boondoggle?" Datamation, vol. 20, no. 3, March 1974, pp. 90, 93-95, 98-99, 102.

Simonton, Wesley. "The Computerized Catalog: Possible, Feasible, Desirable?" Library Resources and Technical Services, vol. 8, Fall 1964, pp. 399-402.

Simpson, H. Clay. "Money Transfer Services." Computers and Society, vol. 7, no. 4, Winter 1976, pp. 3-5, 9.

Simpson, Janice C. "The Cashless Society: Credit it to Capitalism." Black Enterprise, vol. 8, no. 3, October 1977, pp. 42-48.

Sims, Stephen P. "Possible Legal Consequences of the Computer Explosion." Data Processing Magazine, July 1966, pp. 20-26.

Singer, Harold L. "The Hobby Computer Explosion." In Digest of Papers, pp. 216-217. New York, New York: The Institute of Electrical and Electronics Engineers, Inc., Spring COMPCON76, IEEE Catalog No. 76CH1069-4(CR), February 1976.

Singer, J. Peter. "Computer-Based Hospital Information Systems." Datamation, vol. 15, no. 5, May 1969, pp. 38-45.

Sippl, C.J., and Bullen, R. Computers at Large. Indianapolis, Indiana: Bobbs-Merrill, 1976.

Sirbu, Marvin A., Jr. "Automating Office Communications: The Policy Dilemmas." Technology Review, vol. 81, no. 1, October 1978, pp. 50-57.

Sisk, John P. "In Praise of Privacy." Harper's, February 1975, pp. 100-102, 104-107.

Sisson, Roger L., and Canning, Richard C. Computer Applications: A Short Course for Non-EDP Managers. New York, New York: John Wiley and Sons, 1976.

Sitkin, Irwin J. "Touchstone for 2038." Data Management, vol. 16, no. 12, December 1978, pp. 46-49. A home information center, a cashless society, and other predictions.

Skeen, David R. "EDP Certification - Is it Necessary?" AFIPS Conference Proceedings, vol. 43, 6-10 May 1974, pp. 881-888.

Skelly, Stephen J. "Computers and Statute Law." Law and Computer Technology, vol. 3, no. 2, February 1970, pp. 30-41.

Skinner, B.F. "Teaching Machines." Scientific American, vol. 205, no. 5, November 1961, pp. 91-102.

_____. "Why We Need Teaching Machines." Harvard Educational Review, vol. 31, no. 4, Fall 1961, pp. 377-398.

_____. "The Machine that is Man." Psychology Today, vol. 2, no. 11, April 1969, pp. 20, 23-25, 60-63. Condensed from Contingencies of Reinforcement: A Theoretical Analysis.

_____. Beyond Freedom and Dignity. New York, New York: Alfred A. Knopf, Inc., 1971.

Slappey, S.G. "A Lot of People Know Your Secrets." Nation's Business, October 1974, pp. 31-34.

Sloan, Martha E. "The Impact of Digital Technology on Electrical Engineering Education." Proceedings of the IEEE, vol. 66, no. 8, August 1978, pp. 880-885.

Slonneger, Kenneth. "Computer Attitudes." SIGCSE Bulletin, vol. 8, no. 4, December 1976, pp. 26-29.

"Small Firms Exploit Computers More." Minicomputer News, vol. 3, no. 8, 21 April 1977, p. 4.

Smith, August W. "Data Processing Security: A Common Sense Approach." Data Management, vol. 15, no. 5, May 1977, pp. 7-8, 11-13.

Smith, Barry W. "The Economic Impact of Computer-Based Technological Change." Australian Computer Journal, vol. 1, no. 2, May 1968, pp. 65-77.

Smith, Charles P. "Computers, Cops, and Criminals." Datamation, vol. 13, no. 5, May 1967, pp. 61, 63.

Smith, David H. "Scientific Knowledge and Forbidden Truths." Hastings Center Report, vol. 8, no. 6, December 1978, pp. 30-35.

Smith, G.T. "Report on CAI Course in Communication." Poughkeepsie, New York: IBM Corporation, Techincal Report 00.1935, October 1969, 47 pp. On technical writing.

Smith, Robert Ellis. "Take the Privacy Initiative." Computer Decisions, vol. 9, no. 1, January 1977, pp. 35-36.

Smith, Ronald B. "Model for Documenting Controls Strengthens Weak Auditing Link." Data Management, May 1977, pp. 18-22.

Smythe, T. "Data Bank - A New Menace." Labour Monthly, vol. 52, November 1970, pp. 504-509.

Snow, Charles Percy. "Science and the Advanced Society." Computers and Automation, vol. 15, no. 4, April 1966, pp. 14-17.

Sobczak, Thomas V. "Machine Readable Marking Codes: Who Specifies What Type of Symbology?" Computers and People, vol. 27, no. 2, February 1978, pp. 12-21, 23.

Soble, Robert L., and Dallos, Robert E. The Impossible Dream. The Equity Funding Story: The Fraud of the Century. New York, New York: G.P. Putnam's Sons, 1975.

"Some Are Said to Fear Computerized Banking." The Office, vol. 85, no. 5, November 1977, pp. 178-179.

Sorensen, Peter F., Jr., and Burack, Elmer H. "Expanding Computer Technology: Its Roles in Management Development." Personnel Administrator, vol. 23, no. 10, October 1978, pp. 38-42.

Soucek, Branko, and Carlson, Albert D. Computers in Neurobilogy and Behavior. New York, New York: John Wiley and Sons, 1975.

Spangle, C.W. "Minicomputers: Their Expanding Role." Computers and People, vol. 25, no. 12, December 1976, pp. 16-18.

_____. "The Impact of Distributed Systems." *Computers and People*, vol. 26, no. 12, December 1977, pp. 7-10, 27.

Spaniol, Roland, and Smith, Eugene. "The DP Professional and Critical Issues of the Industry." *Data Management*, October 1976, pp. 28-29.

Spencer, Donald D. *Computers in Action: How Computers Work*. Rochelle Park, New Jersey: Hayden Book Company, 1974, 245 pp.

_____. *Computers in Society: The Wheres, Whys and Hows of Computer Use*. Rochelle Park, New Jersey: Hayden Book Company, 1974, 180 pp.

_____. *The Story of Computers*. Ormond Beach, Florida: Abacus Computer Corporation, 1975, 64 pp.

Sperry, W.L. *The Ethical Basis of Medical Practice*. New York, New York: Paul B. Hoeber, Inc., 1950.

Spiro, Kornel. "Computer Systems of the Future." *Management Review*, April 1975, pp. 23-31.

Sprague, Richard E. *Information Utilities*. Englewood Cliffs, New Jersey: Prentice-Hall, Inc., 1969.

_____. "The Invasion of Privacy and a National Information Utility for Individuals." *Computers and Automation*, vol. 19, no. 1, January 1970, pp. 48-49.

_____. "Computer Professionals: What Their Social Concerns Need to Be." *Computers and People*, vol. 24, no. 2, February 1975, pp. 36-39.

_____., and others. "Electronic Funds Transfer Systems: The Sensible Mode of Introduction." *Computers and People*, vol. 27, no. 4, April 1978, pp. 18-22.

Srinivasan, C.A., and Dascher, Paul E. "Computer System Security and Auditing Implications." *National Public Accountant*, vol. 23, no. 1, January 1978, pp. 20-24.

Stafford, John, and Fahey, Noel. "Computer Revolution Puts the Solutions in Manager's Hands." *Saving and Loan News*, vol. 99, no. 5, May 1978, pp. 108-109.

Stake, Robert E. "The Teaching Machine: Tool of the Future or Passing Fancy." *Phi Delta Kappan*, vol. 44, March 1963, pp. 247-249.

Stanford, P. "The Automated Battlefield." *New York Times Magazine*, 23 February 1975, p. 12.

Star, J. "The Computer Data Bank: Will It Kill Your Freedom?" *Look*, 25 June 1968, pp. 27-29.

Startsman, Terry S. "The Attitudes of Medical and Paramedical Personnel Toward Computers." <u>Computers and Biomedical Research</u>, vol. 5, no. 3, June 1972, pp. 218-227.

Stauffer, N. "Instructional Management: Potential Computer Applications." Los Gatos, California: IBM Corporation, Report 16.176, November 1968, 35 pp.

Steel, T.B., Jr. "Artificial Intelligence Research: Retrospect and Prospects." <u>Computers and Automation</u>, vol. 16, no. 1, January 1967, pp. 22-24.

Steely, John E., Jr. "When Management is Automated." <u>Datamation</u>, vol. 24, no. 4, April 1978, pp. 172, 174, 176.

Stehling, Kurt R. <u>Computers and You</u>. New York, New York: New American Library, 1973.

Stein, Karan. "Consumer Reaction to UPC Seen Skeptical." <u>Computerworld</u>, vol. 11, no. 23, 30 May 1977, pp. 2, 12.

Steinberg, Joseph, and Cooper, Heyman C. "Social Security Statistical Data, Social Science Research, and Confidentiality." <u>Social Security Bulletin</u>, October 1967, pp. 3-15.

Steingart, J., and others. "A Comparison of Computer-Assisted Instruction and the Lecture Method of Instruction in Learning to File." Poughkeepsie, New York: IBM Corporation, Technical Report 20.0411, July 1970, 28 pp.

Stent, Gunther S. "The Poverty of Scientism and the Promise of Structuralist Ethics." <u>Hastings Center Report</u>, December 1976, pp. 32-40.

Sterling, Theodor D. "Guidelines for Humanizing Computerized Information Systems: A Report From Standley House." <u>Communications of the ACM</u>, vol. 17, no. 11, November 1974, pp. 609-613.

Sterling, Theodor D., and Laudon, Kenneth. "Humanizing Information Systems." <u>Datamation</u>, vol. 22, no. 12, December 1976, pp. 53-56, 59.

Sterling, Theodor D., and Pollack, Seymour. <u>Computers and the Life Sciences</u>. New York, New York: Columbia University Press, 1965.

Stern, J. "Union View of Automation." <u>Antioch Review</u>, vol. 16, Winter 1956-57, pp. 419-434.

Stern, Les. "Computer Applications vs. Profits." <u>Pensions and Investments</u>, vol. 5, no. 13, 4 July 1977, pp. 3, 21.

Stern, Ludwig. "Security for Your Computer Facility." <u>The Office</u>, vol. 88, no. 2, August 1978, pp. 18-20, 44.

Stessin, Lawrence. "How Private Are Personal Files?" <u>New York Times</u>, Section 3, 9 April 1978, pp. 1, 14.

Stewart, R. *How Computers Affect Management*. Cambridge, Massachusetts: MIT Press, 1972.

Stolurow, Lawrence M. "Computer-Based Instruction." Urbana, Illinois: University of Illinois, Training Research Laboratory, Technical Report 9, July 1965.

Stone, Glenn C., ed. *A New Ethic for a New Earth*. Philadelphia, Pennsylvania: Friendship Press, 1971.

Stoneman, P. *Technological Diffusion and the Computer Revolution*. New Rochelle, New York: Cambridge University Press, 1976.

Strassburger, Fred. "Problems Surrounding 'Informed Voluntary Consent' and Patient Access to Records." *Psychiatric Opinion*, vol. 12, no. 2, February 1975, pp. 30-34.

Strausz-Hupe, Robert. "Social Values and Politics: The Uninvited Guests." *Review of Politics*, January 1968, pp. 59-78.

Streeter, Donald N. *The Scientific Process and the Computer*. New York, New York: John Wiley and Sons, 1974.

"Striking Back at the Super Snoops." *Time*, 18 July 1977, pp. 16-18, 21.

Strother, Robert S. "Crime By Computer." *Reader's Digest*, vol. 108, April 1976, pp. 143-144, 146-148.

Stuart, Robert. "The Social Responsibility of People in Business." *Nation's Business*, vol. 65, no. 4, April 1977, pp. 47-48.

Sturman, Gerald M. "Computers and Urban Society." *Communications of the ACM*, vol. 15, no. 7, July 1972, pp. 652-657.

Sugarman, Robert. "A Second Chance for Computer-Aided Instruction." *IEEE Spectrum*, vol. 15, no. 8, August 1978, pp. 29-37.

_____. "'What's New, Teacher?' Ask the Computer." *IEEE Spectrum*, vol. 15, no. 9, September 1978, pp. 44-49.

_____. "Computers are Making Giant Strides in Automating Production - But Human Decision Making is Still Crucial." *IEEE Spectrum*, vol. 15, no. 10, October 1978, pp. 53-60.

Sullivan, William M. "Cooperating to Establish Disaster Recovery Site." *Data Management*, May 1977, pp. 28-30.

Suppes, Patrick. "Computer Technology and the Future of Eduction." *Phi Delta Kappan*, April 1968, pp. 420-423.

_____. "How Far Have We Come? What's Just Ahead?" *Nation's Schools*, vol. 82, no. 4, October 1968, pp. 52-55. Computer-assisted instruction.

Surden, Esther. "Hammer Tells DPer's of Duties to Society." *Computerworld*, vol. 11, no. 22, 30 May 1977, pp. 1, 6.

Susman, G.I. "Automation, Alienation and Work Group Autonomy." *Human Relations*, vol. 25, April 1972, pp. 171-180.

Susskind, Charles. *Understanding Technology*. Baltimore, Maryland: Johns Hopkins University Press, 1973.

Sutherland, E.H. *White-Collar Crime*. New York, New York: Dryden Press, 1949.

Sutherland, William R. "Impact of Technology on Scientific Publishing." *IEEE Transactions on Professional Communication*, vol. 20, no. 2, September 1977, pp. 56-58.

Swabey, W.C. *Ethical Theory from Hobbes to Kant*. New York, New York: Philosophical Library, Inc., 1961.

Swartz, Boyd G. "Using a Small Computer in the College Mathematics Curriculum." *Educational Technology*, vol. 10, no. 3, March 1970, pp. 31-32.

Szomy, F. "A Commerical Application for a Computer: The Milk Processing Industry." Huntsville, Alabama: IBM Corporation, Report 68-U60-0010, April 1968, 13 pp.

Tamaru, Takuji. "Prospects in Municipal Information Systems: The Example of Los Angeles." *Computers and Automation*, January 1968, pp. 15-18.

Tatham, Laura. *Computers in Everyday Life*. Levittown, New York: Transatlantic Arts, Inc., 1970.

Taube, M. *Computers and Common Sense: The Myth of Thinking Machines*. New York, New York: Columbia University Press, 1961.

Taviss, Irene, ed. *The Computer Impact*. Englewood Cliffs, New Jersey: Prentice-Hall, Inc., 1970, 297 pp.

Taylor, Alan. "In Age of Data Bases, Users Must Check Their Files." *Computerworld*, vol. 10, no. 50, 13 December 1976, p. 15.

_____. "DP Makes it Practical to Evade Information Controls." *Computerworld*, vol. 11, no. 4, 24 January 1977, p. 15.

_____. "Computer-Generated Forms Should be Clear, Legible." *Computerworld*, vol. 11, no. 24, 13 June 1977, p. 59.

Teague, Robert, and Erickson, Clint, eds. *Computers and Society: A Reader*. St. Paul, Minnesota: West Publishing Company, 1974.

Teich, Albert H. *Technology and Man's Future*. New York, New York: St. Martin's Press, 1972.

Teicholz, Eric. "Interactive Graphics Comes of Age." *Datamation*, vol. 21, no. 12, December 1975, pp. 50-53.

Temple, R.H., and Devlin, S.S. "The Use of Microprocessors as Automobile On-Board Controllers." <u>Computer</u>, August 1974, pp. 33-36.

Testerman, Jack D., and Jackson, Juanice. "A Comprehensive Annotated Bibliography on Computer-Assisted Instruction, Part 1." <u>Computer Reviews</u>, vol. 14, no. 10, October 1973, pp. 483-499.

Testerman, Jack D., and Jackson, Juanice. "A Comprehensive Annotated Bibliography on Computer-Assisted Instruction, Part 2." <u>Computer Reviews</u>, vol. 14, no. 11, November 1973, pp. 543-553.

"Texas Instruments Shows United States Business How to Survive in the 1980s." <u>Business Week</u>, 18 September 1978, pp. 66-76.

Thacker, J.B. "The Information Revolution and Social Change." <u>Sixth Australian Computer Conference Proceedings</u>, 20-24 May 1974, pp. 451-467.

"The Application of Computer Technology for Development." New York, New York: United Nations, Publication E/4800 ST/ECA/136, 1971.

"The British Computer Society Code of Good Practice." Manchester, England: NCC Publications, 1972.

"The Coming Battle at the Supermarket Counter." <u>Fortune</u>, September 1975, pp. 105, 182.

"The Coming Boom in Home Computers." <u>Business Week</u>, 16 May 1977, pp. 50D-50E, 50G-50J, 50L-50M, 50O.

<u>The Computer and Invasion of Privacy</u>. United States House of Representatives, Special Subcommittee on Invasion of Privacy, Committee on Government Operations, 89th Congress, 2nd Session, 26-28 July 1966.

"The Computer and Productivity." <u>Computers and People</u>, vol. 24, no. 5, May 1975, pp. 7, 12.

"The Computer Society." <u>Time</u>, vol. 111, no. 8, 20 February 1978, pp. 44-51, 53-59.

"The Computer Thieves." <u>Newsweek</u>, 18 June 1973, pp. 109-112.

"The Computerization of Government Files: What Impact on the Individual?" <u>UCLA Law Review</u>, vol. 15, 1968, pp. 1371-1409.

<u>The Design of a Federal Statistical Data Center</u>. United States House of Representatives, Special Subcommittee on Invasion of Privacy, Committee on Government Operations, 89th Congress, 2nd Session, 26-28 July 1966.

<u>The Fair Credit Reporting Act</u>. United States House of Representatives, Committee on Banking and Commerce, Subcommittee on Consumer Affairs, 91st Congress, 2nd Session, March-April 1970. Hearings.

"The Impact of Automation." *Computer Decisions*, vol. 6, no. 9, September 1974, pp. 37-40.

"The More It Changes, The More It Is the Same Thing." *Computers and People*, vol. 26, no. 9, September 1977, p. 6. Editorial on social responsibility.

"The Privacy Act of 1974." *Data Management*, June 1975, pp. 36-43.

"The Right to Privacy." *Computers and People*, vol. 24, no. 5, May 1975, p. 7.

Theobald, R. "Abundance in Perspective: Should Men Compete with Machines?" *Nation*, vol. 202, 9 May 1966, pp. 544-550.

Thomas, L.J., and others. "Continuous Monitoring of Physiologic Variables with a Dedicated Minicomputer." *Computer*, July 1975, pp. 30-35.

Thomas, Lewis. "Why Can't Computers Be More Like Us?" *Saturday Evening Post*, vol. 248, October 1976, p. 8.

Thompson, Seymour F. "The Invasion of Privacy and Electronic Funds Transfer Systems: Spotlight on the Invaders." *Computers and People*, vol. 25, no. 9, September 1976, pp. 12-13, 19.

Thomson, Judith Jarvis. "The Right to Privacy." *Philosophy and Public Affairs*, vol. 4, no. 4, Summer 1975, pp. 295-314.

Thorne, Peter. "Computer-Assisted Instruction and its Implications for Future Teaching." *Australian Science Teachers Journal*, vol. 16, no. 1, May 1970, pp. 41-44.

Thornton, J. "Office Miracles that Electronics is Bringing." *U.S. News and World Report*, vol. 85, 18 September 1978, pp. 76-78.

"'Threat to Privacy' User...Not Computer." *Electronic News*, 13 March 1967.

Thring, M.W. *Machines: Masters or Slaves of Man*. Herts, England: Peter Peregrinus Ltd., 1974.

Tilly, Charles. "Computers in Historical Analysis." *Computers and the Humanities*, September-November 1973, pp. 323-335.

Tilton, John W. "'Giles Goat-Boy': An Interpretation." *Buckwell Review*, vol. 18, no. 1, Spring 1970, pp. 92-119.

Titus, James P. "The Computer as a Threat to Personal Privacy." *Communications of the ACM*, vol. 9, no. 11, November 1966, pp. 824-826.

_____. "Security and Privacy." *Communications of the ACM*, vol. 10, no. 6, June 1967, pp. 379-380.

Todd, Richard. "You are an Interfacer of Black Boxes." *Atlantic*, March 1970, pp. 64-70.

Toffler, Alvin. *Future Shock*. New York, New York: Random House, 1970, 561 pp.

Tomeski, Edward Alexander. "The Computer Industry's Social Responsibility: A Self-Appraisal." *Computers and People*, March 1975, pp. 6-12, 21.

_____. "The Computer Industry's Social Responsibilities: Another Approach." *Computers and People*, May 1975, pp. 13-15, 31.

_____. "Computers Create Social Issues." *Journal of Systems Management*, vol. 27, no. 2, February 1976, pp. 31-33.

Tomeski, Edward Alexander, and Lazarus, Harold. *People-Oriented Computer Systems: The Computer in Crisis*. New York, New York: Van Nostrand Reinhold Company, 1975.

Tomeski, Edward Alexander; Stephenson, George; and Yoon, B. Man. "Behavioral Issues and the Computer." *Personnel*, vol. 55, no. 4, July-August 1978, pp. 66-74.

Tomeski, Edward Alexander; Wood, Dorothy E.; and Stephenson, George. "2001: A Computer Space Odyssey." *Journal of Systems Management*, vol. 29, no. 4, April 1978, pp. 6-9.

"Too Much Privacy." *Columbia Journalism Review*, January-February 1976, p. 36.

Totten, John K. "Today's EFTS Pilot Projects: Tomorrow's Value Exchange Networks." In *Computers - The Next 5 Years: Digest of Papers*, pp. 125-128. New York, New York: The Institute of Electrical and Electronics Engineers, Inc., Spring COMPCON76, IEEE Catalog No. 76CH1069-4(CR), February 1976.

Toulmin, S. *Foresight and Understanding: An Inquiry into the Aims of Science*. New York, New York: Harper and Row, 1963.

Tritschler, R.J. "Library People and Computer People: Progress and Problems in Communication." Poughkeepsie, New York: IBM Corporation, Technical Report 00.1230, December 1974, 15 pp.

"Trouble in Mass Transit: Why Can't the People Who Put a Man on the Moon get You Downtown?" *Consumer Reports*, vol. 40, no. 3, March 1975, pp. 190-195.

Truitt, W.H., and Solomons, T.W.G. *Science, Technology and Freedom*. Boston, Massachusetts: Houghton Mifflin Company, 1974.

Tsichritzis, Denis. "System Security." Yorktown Heights, New York: IBM Corporation, Report RC-3989, 17 August 1972, 65 pp.

Turing, A.M. "Computing Machinery and Intelligence." *Mind*, vol. 59, 1950, pp. 433-460.

Turn, Rein. *Computers in the 1980s*. New York, New York: Columbia University Press, 1974, 257 pp.

_____. "Privacy Protection in Databanks: Principles and Costs." Santa Monica, California: The RAND Corporation, Report P-5296, September 1974, 21 pp.

_____. "Privacy Systems for Telecommunication Networks." Santa Monica, California: The RAND Corporation, Report P-5292, September 1974, 6 pp.

_____. "Privacy and Security in Centralized vs. Decentralized Databank Systems." Santa Monica, California: The RAND Corporation, Report P-5346, February 1975, 31 pp.

_____. "Cost Implications of Privacy Protection in Databank Systems." Santa Monica, California: The RAND Corporation, Report P-5321, April 1975, 25 pp.

_____. "Privacy Protection and Security in Business Computer Systems." *Atlanta Economic Review*, vol. 26, no. 6, November-December 1976, pp. 24-30.

Turn, Rein, and Ware, Willis H. "Privacy and Security in Computer Systems." Santa Monica, California: The RAND Corporation, Report P-5361, January 1975, 24 pp. Also in *American Scientist*, March-April 1975, pp. 196-203.

Turner, Simon. "Combining Viewdata and the Home Computer Terminal." *Television*, vol. 17, no. 6, November-December 1978, pp. 25-27.

Turoff, Murray, an interview with. "The Future of Computer Conferencing." *The Futurist*, August 1975, pp. 182-190, 195.

Uhlig, Ronald P. "Human Factors in Computer Message Systems." *Datamation*, vol. 23, no. 5, May 1977, pp. 120-126.

Umpleby, Stuart A. "Citizen Sampling Simulations: A Method for Involving the Public in Social Planning." *Policy Sciences*, vol. 1, 1970, pp. 361-375.

_____. "The Teaching Computer as a Gaming Laboratory." *Simulation and Games*, March 1971, pp. 5-25.

_____. "Is Greater Citizen Participation in Planning Possible and Desirable?" *Technological Forecasting and Social Change*, vol. 4, 1972, pp. 61-76. Impact of computer and communication technology on democracy.

"Uncle Sam's Computer Has Got You." *U.S. News and World Report*, vol. 84, no. 14, 10 April 1978, pp. 44-48.

"United States, Petitioner v. Mitchell Miller." Supreme Court of the United States, No. 74-1179, 21 April 1976. Seizure of customer's bank records without a warrant and probable cause.

Urmson, James Opie. *The Emotive Theory of Ethics*. New York, New York: Oxford University Press, 1968.

"Using Computers to Steal - Latest Twist in Crime." U.S. News and World Report, 18 June 1973, pp. 39-40, 42.

Uttal, William R. "On Conversational Interaction." Yorktown Heights, New York: IBM Corporation, Research Paper RC-532, 14 September 1961, 31 pp. Experiments in computerized instruction.

_____. "My Teacher Has Three Arms!!!" Yorktown Heights, New York: IBM Corporation, Research Paper RC-788, 15 September 1962, 42 pp. The instrumentation and programs used in computerized teaching machines.

_____. Real-Time Computers: Techniques and Application in the Psychological Sciences. New York, New York: Harper and Row, Publishers, 1968.

Vail, Hollis. "The Automated Office." The Futurist, vol. 12, no. 2, April 1978, pp. 72-78.

Vallee, Jacques, and others. "The Computer Conference: An Altered State of Communications?" The Futurist, June 1975, pp. 116-121.

Van den Haag, Ernest, and Ross, Ralph. The Fabric of Society. New York, New York: Harcourt Brace Jovanovich, 1957.

Van Tassel, Dennie L. "Advanced Cryptographic Techniques for Computers." Communications of the ACM, vol. 12, no. 12, December 1969, pp. 664-665.

_____. "A Contingency Plan for Catastrophe." Datamation, vol. 17, no. 7, July 1971, pp. 30-33.

_____. Computer Security Management. Englewood Cliffs, New Jersey: Prentice-Hall, Inc., 1972, 220 pp.

_____., ed. The Compleat Computer. Palo Alto, California: Science Research Associates, Inc., 1976, 216 pp.

Vazsony, Andrew. "Information Systems in Management Science." Interface, vol. 3, no. 3, May 1973, pp. 30-33.

Verplank, Joanne Koltnow. "People's Computer Center." In Computer Technology to Reach the People: Digest of Papers, p. 207. New York, New York: The Institute of Electrical and Electronics Engineers, Inc., Spring COMPCON75, IEEE Catalog No. 75CH0920-9C, February 1975.

_____. "Have Micro, Will Travel." Interface, July 1977, pp. 13-16.

Vollmer, H.M., and Mills, D.Z., eds. Professionalization. Englewood Cliffs, New Jersey: Prentice-Hall, Inc., 1966.

von Bertalanffy, L. Robots, Men and Minds. New York, New York: George Braziller, Inc., 1969.

von Foerster, Heintz, and Beauchamp, J.W., eds. Music by Computers. New York, New York: John Wiley and Sons, 1969.

Vonnegut, K., Jr. Player Piano, New York, New York: Holt, Rinehart and Winston, 1952. Science fiction.

von Neumann, J. The Computer and the Brain. New Haven, Connecticut: Yale University Press, 1958.

_____. Theory of Self-Reproducing Automata. Edited and completed by Arthur W. Burks. Urbana, Illinois: University of Illinois Press, 1966.

Wadsworth, M.D. The Human Side of Data Processing Management. Englewood Cliffs, New Jersey: Prentice-Hall, Inc., 1973.

Wagner, Frank V. "Is Decentralization Inevitable?" Datamation, vol. 22, no. 11, November 1976, pp. 86-97.

Wagner, Robert C. "Jury Selection by Computer." Law and Computer Technology, October 1969, pp. 6-11.

Walker, Charles R., ed. Technology, Industry and Man: The Age of Acceleration. New York, New York: McGraw-Hill Book Company, 1968.

Walker, G.M. "Electronic Funds Transfer Systems." Electronics, 24 July 1975, pp. 79-85.

Walker, Terry M. Fundamentals of Computer Science. Boston, Massachusetts: Allyn and Bacon, 1975, 399 pp.

Wallace, Bob. "Community Information Systems." Interface, July 1977, p. 12.

Walter, Donald O. "On Human Dignity and All That." Computers and Society, Winter 1973, pp. 13-14.

Walter, W.G. The Living Brain. New York, New York: W.W. Norton and Company, 1953.

Warburton, Peter. "Human Protests and Objections to the Computer, and the Philosophical Sources of Them." Computers and Automation, vol. 16, no. 10, October 1967, pp. 12-13.

Ward, James A. "The Impact of Computers on the Government." AFIPS Conference Proceedings, FJCC, vol. 27, Part 2, November-December 1965, pp. 37-44.

Ward, Patrick. "Critic Says FAA Control System Has Bugs." Computerworld, vol. 9, no. 10, 7 May 1975, pp. 1-2.

Warden, Benton B. "The Use of Computers in a Local Government Financial Audit." Internal Auditor, vol. 34, no. 1, February 1977, pp. 74-77.

Ware, Willis H. "Computers Unlimited: Digital Machines in Tomorrow's Business World." Santa Monica, California: The RAND Corporation, Report P-434, 21 September 1953, 20 pp.

_____. "The Digital Computer: Where Does it Go from Here?" Santa Monica, California: The RAND Corporation, Report P-608, 5 October 1954, 18 pp.

_____. "Future Computer Technology and Its Impact." Santa Monica, California: The RAND Corporation, Report P-3279, March 1966.

_____. "Security and Privacy in Computer Systems." AFIPS Conference Proceedings, SJCC, vol. 30, 18-20 April 1967, pp. 279-282.

_____. "Security and Privacy - Similarities and Differences." AFIPS Conference Proceedings, SJCC, vol. 30, 18-20 April 1967, pp. 287-290.

_____. Records, Computers, and the Rights of Citizens. Washington, D.C.: United States Department of Health, Education, and Welfare, July 1973.

_____. "Records, Computers, and the Rights of Citizens." Datamation, vol. 19, no. 9, September 1973, pp. 112-114.

_____. "Computer Privacy and Computer Security." Santa Monica, California: The RAND Corporation, Report P-5354, October 1974, 5 pp.

_____. "Legislation Issues Surrounding the Confidentiality of Health Records." Santa Monica, California: The RAND Corporation, Report P-5355, January 1975, 10 pp.

_____. "Privacy: The Private Sector and Society's Needs." Santa Monica, California: The RAND Corporation, Report P-5414, March 1975, 16 pp.

_____. "Testimony Before the National Commission of Electronic Fund Transfer." Computers and Society, Spring 1977, pp. 2-3.

_____. "State of the Privacy Act: An Overview of Technological Social Science Developments." Computers and Society, Spring 1977, pp. 6-9.

_____. "Impact of Telecommunications Technology on the Right to Privacy." Computers and Society, vol. 8, no. 4, Winter 1977, pp. 2-5.

Warfel, George H. "Input Security in Electronic Funds Transfer Systems." In Computer Technology to Reach the People: Digest of Papers, pp. 169-171. New York, New York: The Institute of Electrical and Electronics Engineers, Inc., Spring COMPCON75, IEEE Catalog No. 75CH0920-9C, February 1975.

Waring, John A. "Science for Society." In *Proceedings of the 1972 International Conference on Systems, Man and Cybernetics*, pp. 584-585. New York, New York: The Institute of Electrical and Electronics Engineers, Inc., October 1972.

Warner, M., and Stone, M. *The Data Bank Society*. London, England: George Allen and Unwin, 1970.

Warnock, Geoffrey James. *Contemporary Moral Philosophy*. New York, New York: St. Martin Press, 1967.

Warren, David G. "Computer at Work in State Legislatures." *Law and Computer Technology*, August 1969, pp. 3-9.

Warren, Kenneth. "Freedom of Information: The Cure for the Sickness of Secrecy." *Computers and Industrial Engineering*, vol. 2, no. 4, 1978, pp. 161-162.

Washbrook, H. *Management Control Auditing and the Computer*. London, England: William Heinemann, Ltd., 1971.

Wasserman, Anthony I. "A Problem-List of Public Policy Issues Concerning Computer and Health Care." *Communications of the ACM*, vol. 18, 1975, pp. 279-280.

Waterson, Lynn. "Data Banks Can Protect Privacy." *Banking*, vol. 60, January 1968, p. 56.

Weaver, Paul H. "That Crusade Against Federal Paperwork is a Paper Tiger." *Fortune*, November 1976, pp. 118-121, 206, 208, 210.

Weaver, Warren. "Science and Complexity." *American Scientist*, vol. 36, 1948, pp. 536-544.

Weberman, Ben. "Cash Like a Flash." *Forbes*, 1 April 1977, pp. 42, 45.

Weed, L.L. "Technology Is a Link, Not a Barrier, For Doctor and Patient." *Modern Hospital*, vol. 114, February 1970, pp. 80-83.

Weil, Eric. "Science in Modern Culture, or the Meaning of Meaninglessness." *Daedalus*, vol. 94, no. 1, Winter 1965, pp. 171-189.

Weis, Richard L. "A View of the Future." Poughkeepsie, New York: IBM Corporation, 1 March 1974, 24 pp.

Weisbecker, J. "A Practical, Low-Cost, Home/School Microprocessor System." *Computer*, August 1974, pp. 20-31.

Weiss, E., ed. *Computer Usage/Applications*. New York, New York: McGraw-Hill Book Company, 1970, 313 pp.

Weiss, Harold. "Computer Security: An Overview." *Datamation*, vol. 20, no. 1, January 1974, pp. 42-47.

Weizenbaum, Joseph. "The Two Cultures of the Computer Age." *Technology Review*, vol. 71, April 1969, pp. 54-57.

_____. "On the Impact of the Computer on Society - How Does One Insult a Machine?" *Science*, vol. 176, no. 4035, 12 May 1972, pp. 609-614.

_____. "The Impact of the Computer on Society - Some Comments." *Computers and Automation*, vol. 21, no. 7, July 1972, pp. 18-23.

_____. *Computer Power and Human Reason: From Judgment to Calculation*." San Francisco: W.H. Freeman and Company, 1976, 300 pp.

_____. "Computer Power and Human Reason." *Computers and People*, vol. 25, no. 4, April 1976, pp. 7-12, 26.

_____. "The Last Dream." *Across the Board*, July 1977, pp. 34-46.

_____. "Tools." *ROM*, July 1977, pp. 66-79.

_____., and interview with. "Moral Considerations of Artificial Intelligence." *Personal Computing*, vol. 2, no. 2, February 1978, pp. 21-27.

_____. "Once More - A Computer Revolution." *Bulletin of the Atomic Scientists*, vol. 34, September 1978, pp. 12-19.

_____. "Controversies and Responsibilities." *Datamation*, vol. 24, no. 12, November 1978, pp. 172-173, 176, 179.

Wessel, Andrew E. *Computer-Aided Information Retrieval*. New York, New York: Wiley-Interscience, 1975.

_____. *The Social Use of Information: Ownership and Access*. New York, New York: Wiley-Interscience, 1976.

Wessel, Milton R. *Freedom's Edge: The Computer Threat to Society*. Reading, Massachusetts: Addison-Wesley, 1974, 137 pp.

Westermeier, J.T., and Polin, Kenneth D. "Privacy Report to Alter Relation of Business to the Individual." *Data Management*, vol. 15, no. 9, September 1977, pp. 30-33.

Westin, Alan F. *Privacy and Freedom*. New York, New York: Atheneum, 1967, 487 pp.

_____. "Legal Safeguards to Insure Privacy in a Computer Society." *Communications of the ACM*, vol. 10, no. 9, September 1967, pp. 533-537.

_____. "The Snooping Machine." *Playboy*, May 1968, pp. 130-157.

_____. "Computers and the Protection of Privacy." *Technology Review*, April 1969, pp. 32-37.

_____. "Life, Liberty and the Pursuit of Privacy." *Think*, vol. 35, May-June 1969, pp. 12-21.

_____. "New Laws Will Protect Your Privacy." *Think*, vol. 35, May-June 1969, pp. 27-32.

_____., ed. *Information Technology in a Democracy*. Cambridge, Massachusetts: Harvard University Press, 1971, 499 pp.

_____. "Databanks in a Free Society: A Summary of the Project on Computer Databanks." *Computers and Automation*, vol. 22, no. 1, January 1973, pp. 18-22.

Westin, Alan F., and Baker, Michael A. *Databanks in a Free Society: Computers, Record-Keeping and Privacy*. New York, New York: Quadrangle Books, 1972, 522 pp.

Westin, Alan F., and Berk, Peggy. "The Dimensions of Privacy: A Report on its Status in the United States." *Computers and People*, vol. 28, nos. 7-8, July-August 1979, pp. 2, 14-16.

Westin, Alan F., and Isbell, Florence. *A Policy Analysis of Citizen Rights Issues in Health Data Systems*. Washington, D.C.: U.S. Department of Commerce, National Bureau of Standards Special Publication 469, January 1977.

"What Price Privacy? ... Model Gauges Cost According to Type of System." *Autotransaction Industry Report*, vol. 3, no. 26, 31 March 1976, pp. 4-6.

Wheaton, Bill. "Business Computer Reduces Inventory and Manpower." *The Office*, vol. 87, no. 2, February 1978, p. 77.

Wheeler, Harvey. "Bringing Science Under Law." *The Center Magazine*, vol. 2, no. 2, March 1969, pp. 59-67.

Wheeler, Stanton, ed. *On Record: Files and Dossiers in American Life*. New York, New York: Russell Sage Foundation, 1969.

"When Computers Goof - Consumers Air Their Frustration." *U.S. News and World Report*, 2 May 1977, pp. 61-62.

"Where is the Post Industrial Society Heading?" *International Management*, vol. 32, no. 5, May 1977, pp. 47-48.

Whieldon, David. "How much will 'Privacy' Cost?" *Computer Decisions*, vol. 11, no. 8, August 1979, pp. 54-56, 58, 60, 62.

Whisenand, Paul M., and Hodges, John D., Jr. "Automated Police Information Systems: A Survey." *Datamation*, vol. 15, no. 5, May 1969, pp. 91-96.

Whisenand, Paul M., and Medak, George M. "Security, Justice, and the Computer." *Datamation*, vol. 17, no. 6, June 1971, pp. 24-26.

Whisenand, Paul M., and Tamaru, Tug T. *Automated Police Information Systems*. New York, New York: John Wiley and Sons, 1970.

Whisler, T.L. *The Impact of Computers on Organization*. New York, New York: Pergamon Press, 1970.

White, Lois A. "Computers and Society: Films - An Inventory." *Computers and People*, vol. 25, no. 7, July 1976, pp. 19-22, 26.

White, Peter T. "Behold the Computer Revolution." *National Geographic*, vol. 138, no. 5, November 1970, pp. 593-633.

White, Robert L., and Meindl, James D. "The Impact of Integrated Electronics in Medicine." *Science*, vol. 195, no. 4283, pp. 1119-1124.

Whiteside, Thomas. *Computer Capers: Tales of Electronic Thievery, Embezzlement, and Fraud*. Scranton, Pennsylvania: Thomas Y. Crowell Company, 1978.

Whitlock, James. *Automatic Data Processing in Education*. New York, New York: The Macmillan Company, 1964.

Whyte, William H., Jr. *The Organization Man*. New York, New York: Simon and Schuster, 1956.

Wieczner, Simon. "Interactive Graphics in Design Automation." *Computer*, January 1974, pp. 29-33.

Wiener, Hesh. "Computers and the Future of America." *Computer Decisions*, vol. 9, no. 1, January 1977, pp. 18-19.

_____. "Why Police States Love the Computer." *Business and Society Review*, no. 22, Summer 1977, pp. 38-43.

Wiener, Norbert. *Cybernetics: Or Control and Communication in the Animal and the Machine*. New York, New York: John Wiley and Sons, Inc., 1948.

_____. *The Human Use of Human Beings - Cybernetics and Society*. Boston, Massachusetts: Houghton Mifflin Company, 1950.

_____. "Some Moral and Technical Consequences of Automation." *Science*, vol. 131, no. 3410, 6 May 1960, pp. 1355-1358.

_____. *God and Golem, Inc. - A Comment on Certain Points Where Cybernetics Impinges on Religion*. Cambridge, Massachusetts: MIT Press, 1964.

Wiesner, Jerome B. "Freedom of Information." *Computers and People*, vol. 23, no. 8, August 1974, pp. 26-27.

Wilber, Mike, and Fylstra, David. "Homebrewery vs. the Software Priesthood." *Byte*, October 1976, pp. 90-94.

Wiley, Richard E. "Data Communications: Policies Developing in the United States." *Computers and People*, vol. 25, no. 12, December 1976, pp. 7-9, 21, 26.

Wilkes, M.V. "Can Machines Think?" *Proceedings of the IRE*, vol. 41, October 1953, pp. 1230-1234.

Williams, B. "How Smart are Computers?" *The New York Review of Books*, 15 November 1973, pp. 36-40. Essay on Hubert Dreyfus' book *What Computers Can't Do: A Critique of Artificial Reason*.

Williams, D.Z., and Adams, S. "Computer Technology and Organizational Change." *Management Accounting*, vol. 50, September 1968, pp. 44-48.

Williams, J.D. "Toward Intelligent Machines." Santa Monica, California: The RAND Corporation, Report P-2170, 29 December 1960, 11 pp.

Williams, Robin M., Jr. "Individual and Group Values." *Annals of the American Academy of Political and Social Science*, May 1967, pp. 20-37.

Williams, Theodore J. "The Responsibities of Automating the Office." *The Office*, vol. 85, no. 1, January 1977, pp. 84-85.

Willis, Donald S. "Who Knows You: A Look at Commercial Data Banks." *Computers and Automation*, vol. 22, no. 3, March 1973, pp. 18-21.

Willis, Jerry. *Peanut Butter and Jelly Guide to Computers*. Forest Grove, Oregon: International Scholarly Book Services, Inc., 1978.

Willis, John A. "Is Your Computer Center Safe?" *Computer Decisions*, vol. 4, no. 6, June 1972, pp. 12-14.

Wilson, Andrew. *The Bomb and the Computer: Wargaming from Ancient Chinese to Atomic Computer*. New York, New York: Delacorte, 1968, 218 pp.

Wilson, E.C. "The Knowledge Machine." *Teachers College Record*, vol. 70, no. 2, November 1968, pp. 109-119.

Wilson, I.G., and Wilson, M.W. *What the Computer Cannot Do*. Princeton, New Jersey: Auerbach, 1970.

Winkler, Stanley, and Danner, Lee. "Data Security in the Computer Communication Environment." *Computer*, February 1974, pp. 23-31.

Winograd, Terry. "Artificial Intelligence: When Will Computers Understand People?" *Psychology Today*, May 1974, pp. 73-79.

Winstead, William P. "A Production Computerized Engine Timing Control System." Detroit, Michigan: Society of Automotive Engineers, Inc., Paper 770854, 1977, 7 pp.

Winthrop, Henry. "The Myth of a Coming Age of Leisure." *The Colorado Quarterly*, vol. 22, no. 3, Winter 1974, pp. 343-357.

Wisbey, R.A., ed. *The Computer in Literary and Linguistic Research*. Cambridge, England: Cambridge University Press, 1971.

Withington, Frederick G. *The Real Computer: Its Influence, Uses and Effects*. Reading, Massachusetts: Addison-Wesley Publishing Company, 1969.

_____. "Five Generations of Computers." *Harvard Business Review*, July-August 1974, pp. 99-108.

_____. "Beyond 1984: A Technology Forecast." *Datamation*, vol. 21, no. 1, January 1975, pp. 54-57, 61, 63, 65, 67, 71, 73.

Wohl, Joseph G. "Prospects for Broadband Two-Way Services." In *Proceedings of the 1974 International Conference on Systems, Man and Cybernetics*, pp. 145-149. New York, New York: The Institute of Electrical and Electronics Engineers, Inc., October 1974.

Woodbury, D.O. *Let Erma Do It*. New York, New York: Harcourt Brace, 1956. Automation and its consequences.

Wooldridge, Dean E. "Can Mechanical Man Find Goodness, Truth and Beauty?" *Psychology Today*, vol. 2, no. 11, April 1969, pp. 26, 28-29, 64.

Wooldridge, Susan, and London, Keith. *The Computer Survival Handbook - How to Talk Back to Your Computer*. Boston, Massachusetts: Gambit Incorporated, 1973.

Wooton, Leland. "The Emergence of Multinational Information Centers." *Management International Review*, vol. 17, no. 4, 1977, pp. 21-34.

_____. "The Mangerial Implications of Multinational Information Centers." *Management International Review*, vol. 18, no. 2, 1978, pp. 77-85.

"Would You Buy a Used Computer from This Man?" *Forbes*, 15 March 1977, p. 104.

Wright, Van O. "Computer-Aided Instruction: My Teacher, the Computer." *Training*, vol. 14, no. 9, September 1977, pp. 56-57.

Yarbrough, L. Everett. "The Florida Project: A System for Processing Educational Data Electronically." *Journal of Educational Data Processing*, vol. 3, Spring 1966, pp. 58-66.

Yasaki, Edward K. "France is Ready to Clamp Down on Computer Abuses of Privacy." *Datamation*, vol. 23, no. 4, April 1977, pp. 162-165.

Yoder, Richard D. "Management of Computer Failures in Clinical Care." *Datamation*, vol. 18, no. 10, October 1972, pp. 78-80, 82.

Young, Elmer D. "Data Bank for Narcotics Addicts." *Computers and Automation*, vol. 19, no. 10, October 1970, pp. 40-42.

Young, Whitney M., Jr. "Intermingled Revolutions: The Negro and Automation." *Vital Speeches of the Day*, vol. 30, 1 September 1964, pp. 692-694.

Yourdon, Edward. "Maybe the Computers Can Save Us After All." *Computers and Automation*, vol. 20, no. 5, May 1971, pp. 21-26. A possible National Information Bureau.

Zaiden, Dennis J. "Some Legal Aspects of EDP." *Management Accounting*, July 1972, pp. 51-52.

Zalud, Bill. "Evolving Electronic Funds Transfer Means Vital Societal Alternations." *Data Management*, vol. 15, no. 3, March 1977, pp. 18-20.

_____. "Meeting the Ultimate Disaster." *Data Management*, vol. 15, no. 5, May 1977, p. 30.

Zampolli, Antonio. "Humanities Computing in Italy." *Computers and the Humanities*, vol. 7, no. 6, September-November 1973, pp. 343-360.

Zani, Ralph L., and Zani, William M. "Toward the Computer Utility: Evolution and Revolution." *Datamation*, vol. 15, no. 10, October 1969, pp. 125-132.

Zani, William M. "Blueprint for MIS." *Harvard Business Review*, vol. 48, no. 6, November-December 1970, pp. 95-100.

Zannetos, Zenon S. "New Directions for Management Information Systems." *Technology Review*, vol. 71, October-November 1968, pp. 35-39.

Zeitlin, Lawrence R. "The Ultimate Personal Computer." *Datamation*, vol. 23, no. 5, May 1977, pp. 131-132, 137.

Zemanek, H. *The Skyline of Information Processing*. New York, New York: Elsevier-North Holland, 1972.

Zimmerman, David R. "An Ethical Dilemma: Patient Privacy vs. His Insurability." *Modern Medicine*, 28 October 1974, pp. 18-24. About the Medical Information Bureau.

Zinn, Karl L. "Instructional Uses of Interactive Computer Systems." *Datamation*, vol. 14, no. 9, September 1968, pp. 22-27.

_____. "Instructional Programming Languages." *Educational Technology*, vol. 10, no. 3, March 1970, pp. 43-46.

_____. "Computer in the Instructional Process: Direction for Research Development." *Communications of the ACM*, vol. 15, no. 7, July 1972, pp. 648-651.

Zobrist, Albert L., and Carlson, Frederic, R., Jr. "An Advice-Taking Chess Computer." *Scientific American*, vol. 228, no. 6, June 1973, pp. 92-105.

Zussman, Ronald, and others. "Towards an Automated Stock Exchange." *Computer Decisions*, vol. 6, no. 1, January 1974, pp. 24-27.